HOW YOU BEAR IT

TRIUMPH AND RESILIENCY IN LIFE

BY TOM DEBLASS
WITH LOUIS MARTIN

Printed in the United States of America
Print ISBN: 978-1-956019-35-3
eBook ISBN: 978-1-956019-34-6

Published by DartFrog Blue, the traditional publishing imprint of DartFrog Books.

Publisher Information:
DartFrog Books
4697 Main Street
Manchester, VT 05255
www.DartFrogBooks.com

It does not matter what you bear,
but how you bear it.
—Seneca

Dedicated to my father, wait for me in heaven.

ACKNOWLEDGEMENTS

Tom: My father, for teaching me so many life lessons. Without him, there's no book and certainly no me. My mother, for being a true rock and an example of strength for the whole family. To my children, Tom and Isabelle, my life and my reason for breathing. Gordon and the team at DartFrog for being patient with my crazy life and schedule.

Of course, thank you to Louie, equal parts writer, friend, and counselor. I don't know what he thought he was getting into, but I pulled him deep into my past and relived some pain that I would never have otherwise. He had front-row seats to one of the craziest years of my life and I didn't scare him off. He asked the hard questions and never stopped writing, even as I watched my father pass.

Louie: I'd like to thank Tom, first and foremost. Writing a book is hard, but the control you give up when co-writing is harder. In our lives, there will be a handful of people that we see the "real" version of. I saw Tom's; it's a privilege that I didn't take lightly.

I'd also like to thank Roy Billington for making the connections and putting my name out there. This book was his idea. I imagine he's as surprised as I am to be actually reading these words. To Gordon and the team at DartFrog Books, who trusted us that this little world of combat sports was worth writing about.

Finally, my wife, Sara, who listened patiently and helped absorb some of the impacts of this story, often while holding a newborn in one hand.

CO-AUTHOR NOTE

This book is the product of a year of interviews between Tom DeBlass and his co-author. Memories are imperfect; everyone knows that. Everything from small details to specific dates and orders of events may get changed, completely unintentionally. Tom has accumulated more memories and relationships in his years than most people do in a lifetime. There's simply more to remember.

Every story in this book was recalled, retold, put down on paper, reviewed, and likely rewritten. That's a lot of steps, and in any one of them details can be lost in translation. We've done our best to get everything right, keeping the spirit of the story intact. All of the big moments and events are correct. But some of the smaller details may not be. In places where we came up short, the fault lies squarely with the co-author. Stories are messy and imperfect. So is telling them.

PROLOGUE

I pull up to the sidewalk. I won't be here that long. I never honk, not wanting to wake up the neighborhood this early, plus it would just seem rude to my rider. Instead, I send him a text message.

Here.

The screen door opens up; a dog barks somewhere down the street. The real working class have already left for their jobs in the city, but moms in Jersey are still running their kids around to get them fed and ready for the buses.

I like this time of the morning, just after dawn. You can get a lot done this time of day, when the world is still bleary-eyed. I'm no exception. I got a full four hours of sleep. It's a good average for me. I've struggled with insomnia all my life. I don't know why I like mornings; they're actually hell for me. One of the many ways I make my life harder than it needs to be.

My car door opens with a dull latching sound, and a little bell rings somewhere to alert me that someone is getting in. The old man takes short, precise steps so as not to lose his footing. He's dressed as casually as me, gray sweatpants and a hoodie. I briefly feel the cold draft from outside pushing into the heated comfort of my truck. You have to work to be physically uncomfortable in this thing. Heated seats, dual AC, everything adjustable. Plenty of room, plenty of buttons to dial everything in. It's a bit much, but I think I've earned it after driving shit cars for so many years. Plus, I spend a lot of time driving, and I'm frequently in pain from one thing or another. A comfortable car makes all the difference.

The old man slips on the step up and winces in pain. My eyes shoot down to his feet. He has really bad feet. I regret admiring my truck for a second. But he recovers quickly.

"I think it rained last night," he says, to shift the blame for his slippage.

I just grunt an affirmative and sip my coffee. I wait for him to get settled in, then we roar off in my tank of a truck. It's a twenty-minute drive to our destination. Most days we talk—mostly small talk, but sometimes meaningful stuff. It's all meaningful, really. It's not always the conversation but the time that matters. Who knows how much time we have left?

"The kids wanted to come over this weekend," I say.

"Sure. Deb was going to try her casserole again."

We both laugh. It's an inside joke that her casserole is terrible.

"Naw, I'll talk her into pizza," says the old man. We're at a point where I don't even ask about the kids coming over; I just say they're coming and they do. They love the old man, and he loves them. It's important to me, enough that it's not worth telling them anything more than they need to know about him. Does anything else really matter? He's a good grandpa, that's all they need to know.

My dad goes quiet and browses around the interior. He blinks a few times at the onboard display, trying to make sense of it all. He looks at the ugly metal dog tags hanging off my rear-view mirror. Finally his eyes drift on and land at a small stack of papers in the middle seat. Even from a distance, they look official, with small fonts and dense paragraphs. My dad is smart and a little nosey at times, and he plucks the papers up and flips through them.

"What's this?"

"It's, ahh, a contract. There's this thing called ONE FC—"

"What kind of contract?" he says in his thick Jersey accent while reading.

"There's this thing called ONE FC—"

"For a fight?"

"Yeah, these guys from—"

"Ahh!" he says while pointing at the paper. "ONE FC. I've heard of them," he says as his eyes keep skimming through the contract.

"What are they, like the Chinese UFC?"

"No, Dad, they're based in . . . in . . . they're not Chinese, Dad."

He waves his hand dismissively, which is good because I don't win many geography arguments. "I thought you weren't ever fighting again."

"I changed my mind," I say truthfully, but maybe a little defensive as well.

"Changed your mind," he repeats with a nod. He lowers the papers and looks at me. "So you're going to fight in China? When?"

"Hong Kong, in October."

"Where?"

"Hong Kong."

"I thought you said it was China?"

"No, *you* said it was China. I'm saying Hong Kong."

"Aren't they the same thing?" Dad says with an annoying tone.

"I dunno, I think they're different, technically."

Our voices are raising slightly.

"But you're fightin' Chinese people?"

"Maybe, I don't know. They have fighters from everywhere. Could be a guy from the U.S."

We're both waving our hands in the air by now to punctuate our sentences. There's a brief pause as I pull up to the parking lot.

"All right," he says, bringing the conversation to an abrupt end. He waits for the truck to stop and then climbs out, still holding the stack of papers.

I lean over and call out to him, "Hey, I need that back."

"I'll bring it back," he says while walking. He notices my perturbed look and repeats himself with a more convincing tone. "I'll bring it back."

I sit back in the car, wondering why I let him walk away with what I'm supposed to read until he gets back.

Twenty minutes later, I see him walking out of the building and back to the car, albeit a little slower. His limp is gone, or lessened. He opens the truck door and slides on in.

"That's it, then," he says. He eases into the seat and sinks low, his gut popping out comfortably, and he sighs. I look at him, amused, and say, "Comfortable?"

He doesn't answer. Instead he takes a rolled-up and wrinkled stack of papers from his pocket, something I'm sure was my nice, neat contract that I need to fax back to ONE FC this morning after class. He slaps it on my lap like it's a newspaper with a shocking headline.

"It's a province."

"Sometimes I think you're a province," I joke.

It fires him up, and he motions with his hands excitedly at the contract. "No, smartass, Hong Kong. It's what they call a province. It's like Puerto Rico is to us."

"Is that so?" I decide not to bust his balls about it too much. I can tell when he's just repeating something, probably from the lady he flirts with in the clinic. I pull out of the parking lot. The day is officially begun, the sun is out, and the streets are filling up with some latecomers to work.

"I think it's a great idea, you fighting again."

"Oh yeah, coming around, huh?" I say it playfully, but Dad's mood shifts abruptly.

"Yeah, well, you know, Tom . . ." He takes a breath and continues. "You still got a lot of fire, and I, uh, think you could put together another run."

I smile, a little touched by the sentiment. "Well, as long as my Dad believes in me. I need to introduce you to some people on Reddit."

"What's red it? No no, it doesn't matter. Thomas, look. I mean this."

I take my eyes off the road and look at him, surprised to see his eyes watering up. I wonder if it's just the medication, if it makes him more emotional. After all, we're just talking.

"I have a lot of regrets; you know that."

I just nod, and he continues. "And I never . . . I missed a lot when you were coming up."

Reflexively, I say, "No Dad, it's not your fault. You gotta understand—"

He motions me to stop with his hand. "No no no, listen. I can own that. I missed a lot of your life, or I was in and out. You know what I mean."

We start talking over each other. I tell him, "You were dealing with your own demons—"

"I feel like I don't even know your story. I mean I got *some* stuff, but it's like there's whole parts missing, you know?"

We drive in silence for a few seconds. I wonder if the outburst is over, then scold myself for thinking about it in that way. So many parents in this world don't give a shit about their kids. Here's my dad telling me he wishes he could know more.

I clear my throat. "Well, what do you want to know? I can tell you."

He takes a second. "I wanna know everything, the whole thing."

We pull back up to the house. The truck stops, but he stays in his seat.

He speaks again. "I have questions, things I never asked. Things I should have known."

Another long silence as we both process the moment. I finally take the offer. "I'll be here tomorrow, same time. It's a twenty-minute drive there and back. I'm an open book for that time."

He nods without looking at me. "Okay, okay. I'd like that." He turns and places his hand on the door but stops to say, "What time on Saturday? With the kids?"

I drive to the gym for my morning class, in deep thought. It's strange for my Dad to want to know my story. He was there for the whole thing. I've talked to him nearly every day for my entire life. What he remembers is another story. My father was always there, and yet often somewhere else. It's not hard to explain, but it's not easy to understand either.

I go about my day like normal, taking some comfort in my routine. Class, rolling, mitt work, cool-down. The physicality, the self-inflicted harshness. I've always found release in pain, in ordeal. Adversity is important, suffering is important. For so many things in my life that never truly got solved, I learned that endurance was the next best thing. It's a lesson I learned from my parents, both father and mother.

I finish the last classes of the evening. Walking to my truck in my shorts and sandals, I smell like dried sweat, and the cold Jersey air feels amazing to my overheated body. I drive home, still under the influence of the euphoria of jiu-jitsu and hard physical activity. I wonder what my life could have been like without it, even though I know the answer. It would have been bad, it's just a matter of how creative I can get in my head. On a scale of one to my father, how bad could it have gotten? I love my father, warts and all. I don't just love him, I accept him. So it doesn't bother me to acknowledge that his life could have easily been waiting for me had I not made some key choices.

I walk in the door, and my kids tackle me with laughter and excitement. The best feeling in the world, better than all the medals, all the DVD sales, all the black belts. My daughter asks, "Can we go see Grandpa tomorrow?"

"Oh, 'course," I say, and they throw their hands up in glee, then pepper me with a hundred questions and stories about their days.

CHAPTER 1

I pick my Dad up Monday, curious if he will even acknowledge the conversation from last week now that the weekend has passed and the grandkids came over. He didn't mention it at all when I dropped them off or picked them up. People get emotional, especially with some methadone in their system. My father is like me, he's passionate. God knows I've said some things in the heat of the moment. Men in particular are exceptional at spectacular displays of emotion, followed by denial that it happened at all.

Still, some part of me is hopeful. Maybe he will remember; maybe it wasn't just a one-way confession that he needed to make, only to disregard later. Maybe he actually needs this, to hear his son's story.

He slides into the car in his grey sweatpants and sweater. He looks like he doesn't have a care in the world. I appraise him carefully as we start our drive. We have some small talk for the first fifteen minutes. We talk about my son, how he's getting big, how he's learning this or that. My father seems a bit distant. His voice trails off once or twice.

We pull up to the clinic and he leaves the car with a mumble that he'll be back. I sit in the car alone, disappointed. It triggers some powerful memories, none of them good. My father always loved me growing up, but for many important moments of my life, I can't find him when I search my memories. If love is a series of chemical reactions in your brain, whatever power they have over you pales in comparison to the chemicals of addiction—a cocktail of compulsion that leaves you passed out, in and out of consciousness for days when your kids are graduating junior high or something. I guess it felt like when push came to shove, the chemicals always won. Maybe this is the wrong way to look at this, but it feels like they won again, by making him say something he didn't mean, or meant but didn't plan to follow through with.

I sit in silence with my own thoughts in the truck for a long time until I hear a clicking sound. I snap back to the now. My father is trying to open the door, but it's locked. I let him in and he proceeds to bust my balls.

"UFC fighter locking his doors now?"

"Trying to keep *you* out."

He gives a laugh, although I was only half joking. I start the truck and stew for most of the drive home.

"So where do you want to start?" he says abruptly.

"Start?"

He stares at me for a second. I'm not sure who should go first.

"The talking! The story! You had the whole thing in here with the crying," he barks out.

"I had it? *You* were the one with all that."

"It was you, it was me, whatever. Let's get this thing started."

"It was definitely you."

He grunts a noise I can only interpret as a tacit admission of guilt but keeps right on going.

"I mean, I'm not asking for a fucking biography here. I mean I was there."

"So no, like, 'I was born on this day.' Nothing like that."

He waves his hand dismissively, "What's there to say?"

He goes quiet and moves to scratch an itch on his head. His eyes fall to the floor as two decades of complicated memories flash in both of our heads.

"What's there to say?" he repeats, less convincingly now.

We awkwardly agree to begin during another time, unspecified but clearly well after my childhood. It's just as well. Truthfully, there is *everything to say* about how I grew up. And as for my father's claim that he was there for the whole thing:

He was, and he wasn't.

———•———

I come from a family with its share of hardship on both sides. I'm talking about generational tragedy.

My father, Tom senior, is a good man but a complicated one. He was everything a good father should be. He came to school things, he kissed my Mom, he was a hard worker. My dad was affectionate; I always felt loved.

He didn't fit the profile of a typical alcoholic, if there is such a thing. To this day I get odd looks from people when I tell them I had a great dad and, in the next breath, say he struggled with addiction my entire life. My father using wasn't a different man as much as he was no man at all. His drugs of choice were all downers, and he would just sort of fade away. Some people get loud and belligerent under the influence, but my father was more likely to pass out on a couch for a few hours and then walk around in a haze. He was remarkably self-aware about this. On more than one occasion growing up, he explained to me that he was an alcoholic. What's more, he didn't use it as an excuse. He would apologize later for things he said and did while under the influence.

Many alcoholics split themselves into two people. They tell themselves they are a good guy. It's that *other guy*, the one with the drinking problem, that's the monster. Or maybe the booze is the monster, inhabiting your body and forcing you to do terrible things. My dad wasn't a coward. He took responsibility for his addictions.

With that said, there are no good addicts. First off, his addiction didn't end with alcohol. Over the years, my father struggled with narcotics of all kinds. Some of it was pills, to cope with injuries that caused him pain. There's no excuses for what he did. But there's a difference between excuses and reasons. My father suffered a severe vertebrae injury when I was young. As the breadwinner in the family, he had to work. Period. He did what he had to do. People were far more ignorant of the dangers of painkillers and opioids back then. They were easy to get, and just as hard to quit.

He was strong, mentally and physically. All the men in my family were. My grandfather was a mountain of a man. He may have been the source of the DeBlass temper, or maybe just the last known inheritor from his own father. He would run people off the road who'd cut him off. He would drag them out of cars and manhandle them while my Dad looked on in the passenger seat. This behavior would land a man in a court today, but then it was a minor event in the life of a New Jersey resident. He was stronger than my father, and my father was stronger than me. They both had the kind of strength that doesn't come from doing three sets of ten on a gym machine. Their strength was from living hard. They weren't toned or jacked, but I saw my grandfather bend a railroad spike with his bare hands one time. And my father, I remember watching him one night getting progressively more drunk as the hours went by. He went into our backyard where there was a pile of bricks. I mean actual bricks used for construction. I remember him propping one up on a chair and shattering it with a punch. And not just one, either; he could smash several bricks if he had enough to drink. I remember being in awe of that as a child. Now, the memory is more conflicted. What kind of pain would a man have to be in to do that to himself?

My father began drinking when he was twelve, and his father was a functioning alcoholic as well. They lived in an era when alcoholism was barely acknowledged. There were few books, fewer treatment centers, and no hotlines. Alcohol was the socially accepted way to cope. I got hints over the years that my father . . . let's just say he had plenty of things to cope with.

You might think a man like this wouldn't tolerate weakness in a son. But, again, he wasn't the typical alcoholic. When I would come home crying because the neighborhood kids picked on me, a sober Dad was always there to comfort me. I was free to cry around him. He would do what every Dad should do: get on one knee and wrap his arms around me. He'd tell me it was okay, ask me what happened, and do all that good-Dad stuff that I try to do with my kids now.

In reality, I know my Dad wasn't really two people. That's something that children of addicts just sort of need to believe sometimes. Separate the man from the addict. My father was a good person. But he was a complex person. Mentally strong and yet hopelessly addicted. Tender with his son, but able to smash bricks. Not surprisingly, I had many of these same traits from a young age.

My mother, Debra, was on the other side of the DeBlass coin. She was then and is now the strongest, toughest woman I've ever met in my life. Sometimes I think she deserves a book more than me. My childhood wasn't always easy, but it paled in comparison to hers. Debra was born in East Orange, New Jersey, a mainly black neighborhood. And by "mainly" I mean Debra was the only white girl in her high school. Savvy history readers may note that Debra would have been in the correct time and place for the 1967 race riots in New Jersey, and she was. But that was almost a footnote in her life story. Debra's mother was born and raised in an orphanage. With no family of her own, I can't blame my grandmother for not being a stellar parent. She married an alcoholic, and the two had a turbulent marriage. My mother was kidnapped when she was five or six and wasn't reunited with her family for years. Her kidnapper was none other than her own father, a severe alcoholic himself. He took not just my mother but her infant brother as well. You might imagine that Debra's mother would have moved heaven and earth to find her children. But she never really made a serious effort to find them.

With a mother who wasn't coming for them and a father who could barely keep himself together, Debra raised her little brother like a son. She never was able to be a child. Her father would sometimes take them to a bar and leave them in the car until morning while he would get drunk. Adversity, even tragedy, was normalized for my mother. But instead of breaking her, it caused her to develop a sort of pathological sense of kindness and empathy. She would do anything for me, her son. What's remarkable is that she would probably do those same things for strangers.

Years later, my mother developed a rare condition called trigeminal neuralgia, which causes excruciating pain in the face from even the lightest touches. If you can, imagine being a little kid and watching your mom putting makeup on, and then she abruptly cries out in pain and collapses on the floor like a wounded animal. It was a regular occurrence growing up for me. It was completely unfair that such an amazing woman would draw the short genetic straw. But, if anything, it made her more of a hero in my eyes. Debra learned to live with it. She didn't complain; she didn't quit on life.

They were an interesting pairing, Tom and Debra. They were so different, and yet they both understood hardship and struggle. It's an odd thing to be united around, but it worked in our family. People ask me sometimes why my mother didn't leave my father on account of his addictions. The answer is that my mother had lived with flawed people her entire life. She didn't have a recognizable version of normal that most people have in their families. But also, she truly loved my father through it all. And she still does.

It was largely the same with me. Every day I saw suffering in my home. My father's drinking and depression. My mother's fits of pain. I settled into the role of peacemaker and comforter almost from the time that I could speak. It was a lot to put onto a child, too much. When I was about four years old, I saw my Dad overdose. He was splayed out on a carpet, and my mother sat in front of him, trying to wake him up. When it was clear that he wouldn't, my mother let out a wail of pain and began sobbing. We thought he was dead. This happened more than once when I was a child.

Around the second grade a teacher began to remark that I wasn't like the other kids. Even back in the '80s, it wasn't hard to diagnose me as depressed. My school referred me to some sort of psychologist. I'll never forget the first and only time I met with him. By the end of our session, he literally had nodded off to sleep.

I never saw a professional again, but the depression didn't go away.

I remember sitting outside my house on the curb, praying every night that my father would stop drinking, that my mother would be cured of her pain. I would sit by myself under a streetlight and pray.

This was the family I was born into. Surprisingly, I was generally a nice kid. Unfortunately the neighborhood I grew up in was anything but nice. New Jersey in any decade isn't Disneyland. But in the early 1980s, it was probably one of the least desirable places to live in the country. There was a terrible recession; unemployment was above ten percent in the U.S. New York City was the most dangerous city in the country and had some of the highest murder rates in the Western world throughout the decade. It was ground zero for the crack epidemic. On the doorstep of all of this was New Jersey. My neighborhood wasn't a war zone. People weren't dying on the streets. But tough times breed tough people. And tough kids. If you weren't a tough kid in Bayville, the other kids would *make* you tough.

I was always the runt of the neighborhood. I was the four-year-old trying to play with ten-year-olds. Half the kids I grew up with had their own family issues. But whereas I was a nice kid, a lot of the older boys were not. Even well-behaved boys will beat the shit out of each other for fun. But a ten-year-old from a broken home may do it to release anger from issues he doesn't even know about yet. And who do you think he'll target? That's right, the smallest kid on the block. That was me.

I feel like the first several years of my life was other kids beating the shit out of me. If you can, imagine a five-year-old getting in fistfights with eight- and ten-year-olds. When you're five, advanced kids your age will be able to do things like walk up and down stairs and stand on one foot. When I was five, I got my first concussion.

I remember very clearly this kid who tortured me in the neighborhood. I don't know what his problem was. But, like I said, it was 1980s New Jersey, so it could have been anything. Broken home, addict parent, or maybe just born bad. Like most kids, he was probably five or six years older than me. He wasn't the only bully, but he's the one that I remember. There was this sand pit at the end of our block where the kids would all hang out. They would throw me in, jump on me, and hit me. They made me eat dirt or smashed my head against trees. Me, a five year old. A kid like that can't even process complex emotions yet.

One day a bunch of us were "playing." We didn't have slides or monkey bars. So we reverted to basic boy stuff: we found rocks and threw them at things. Of course, we eventually started throwing them at each other. In the beginning, we just threw them at each other's feet. But, being boys, we were hardwired for warfare. Before long this kid, who already had a hard-on for me being the smallest and weakest target available, was gleefully throwing rocks at my face as hard as he could. He was a little serial killer in the making; he legitimately got off on watching me be terrified. I remember being on my hands and knees, asking him to stop as he searched for another rock to throw. The pretense of any sort of a game was gone by then. He wasn't even throwing them at me as much as he was just dropping them on my head at point-blank range.

I had some sort of realization that this kid would not stop; he would keep doing this forever. If I survived today, he would just be there tomorrow and the next day. It wasn't fair. Suddenly, I was standing up with a rock in my hand. A big one. And not a smooth rock like you find on a river in the country. This was a jagged lump of wrecked New Jersey concrete, the kind of rock that scraped up your hand just by picking it up. As my bully closed within arm's distance, I threw a haymaker at him as hard as I could. The punch alone might have rattled him. It hit him directly on the ear. But with the rock of Jersey justice in my hand, it did quite a bit more than that.

His ear exploded, a combination of the cartilage being burst by the blunt force of the rock and the skin being torn open by its jagged edges. Instead of swelling his ear up, all the fluid the body sent to the ear to protect it gushed out. It was clearly the kind of injury that was out of our league, beyond what we should have been inflicting on each other. Of course, I had literally had a concussion two months before and none of the kids seemed to give a shit. But the graphic nature of what that rock did to this kid's face was probably a little bit more than we had seen so far in our little Jersey block.

Everyone froze for a few seconds to register. Well, except for my bully. He regressed from whatever age he was back to a toddler, screaming bloody murder. He crumpled to the ground and curled up in a pitiful little ball of dirt and blood. That's what he probably was anyways, just a frustrated toddler at heart. I'll never forget the other kids staring down at this bully, now crumpled on the sand, holding his ear. He had lost one hundred percent of his power. He could come back the next day and try and hurt every single one of us, but he would never be the same. One you've seen a person shrunken into the fetal position, that's all you'll ever see when you look at them. His hand was caked with blood and dirt, and more blood was steadily dripping out, making more of a mess by the second. They looked from him up at me. A paradigm shift occurred for everyone in that sand pit. Don't mess with Tom anymore.

I was never bullied again. It was a powerful lesson for me. Bullies have to work hard. They're in the business of fear, and you can never let up in that business. But a bully only needs to get beaten once, and if it's bad enough and enough people see it, they lose that power forever.

CHAPTER 2

We pull up to the clinic after a few moments in silence. Perhaps we're both having a gut-check moment. I'm not telling him these stories to twist the knife.

I try to throw him an easy out. "Hey, you know, we don't have to talk about these things."

No reply.

I continue: "It's not to make you or anybody feel bad. You know that, right? You were a good Dad. You *are* a good Dad."

He stares down at the floorboard and nods to himself. He says softly, "When I showed up."

I don't say anything. It's almost like he's having a conversation with himself that I don't want to interrupt. We sit in the parking lot in silence.

"You're showing up now," I finally say.

"Yeah," he replies with a shaky voice. He abruptly opens the door and steps out, leaving me alone with my thoughts while he heads into the clinic. Maybe this was a mistake. I realize that I've always told my parents about what happened to me, but not always about how it *felt* while it happened. Maybe in some ways, I never thought much about it anyways. The feelings, that is.

He returns to the car and lets out a sigh. "So what happens next?"

"Umm, where were we? Maybe right before I met—"

"I wanna know it all. Every minute," he says firmly.

"Yeah, I know. I just don't want you to think—"

"Hey, look at me."

I look at him, and he slowly lifts his finger and points at the ground.

"Every. Minute."

My Dad may say he wants to know every minute of my life. But he doesn't. Just like I don't need to know every moment of his. There are some things that no one needs to know; they would only cause more pain. I've come to peace with what happened to me, but that peace didn't come overnight.

I was seven years old when it happened. He was thirteen. He molested me just one time, in his room. It's hard to understate how unprepared an eight-year-old is for sexual activities. I had no real understanding of sexuality, certainly not the particulars. But more than that, I had a limited understanding of emotions of any kind, and I didn't even have the words in my vocabulary to understand or vocalize what happened. What I did have was the most damaging thing: a very simplistic understanding of morality. What happened to me was complicated. A child, who was very likely himself being abused, abused another child. It's hard to say what level of culpability, or even understanding, he had of what he was doing. These are the types of things that legal systems and even philosophers would struggle with. But my seven-year-old mind couldn't discern any of this. Instead, I went into emotional retreat, one that would last well into my adult life, for years. To this day I think of that child who molested me. He was a victim; he was in his own emotional retreat from someone else.

But he still did it, and I was never the same.

In the immediate aftermath, I felt enormous guilt and shame. I read stories about Sodom and Gomorrah from the Bible. God had destroyed entire cities over homosexuality. A narrative emerged in my mind about what *we* had done, not what *he had done to me*. Molestation was something that the creepy old man down the street did. Having it done to me by another young boy confused me. I didn't know what to call it, how to describe it. I was seven years old.

For these reasons, I told no one.

Boys typically become aware of sex between the ages of ten and twelve. I was considerably younger, and the idea of sex was always wrapped up in the context of this terrible thing in a dark corner of my mind. As I approached high school, I was dating frequently. I was athletic, I had a personality, and I wasn't ugly. It was enough to clear the low bar for teenage relationships.

I had sex with a girl when I was very young, maybe fifteen. Then another girl, and another. I developed a bit of a reputation amongst the girls at school, and it was a good one. I was an experienced guy relative to other boys. I treated women kindly, because of my saintly mother. And most importantly: I didn't tell anyone. I was a no-drama guy. No slut-shaming, no vicious breakups, not even locker-room talk. I had been hiding my sexuality since I was eight, and it continued.

As this happened, I discovered another effect from being molested, the one that would be the hardest to be free of for the rest of my life: I had difficulty feeling intimate with girls. When I was a teenager, boys and girls were falling in and out of love at the drop of a dime, soaring into the heights of passion on Monday only to end the week in a downward spiral of mistrust and despair about their partner's activities. I simply could not. I had three girls tell me they loved me in high school. I couldn't love any of them, even if I wanted to love all three.

At the same time, I was not unable to feel empathy. I had a strong sense of justice, and I was protective of people I felt were being mistreated. To kids being picked on constantly, I was a rare find. No underdog was too good for me to stick up for.

But with girls, and later women, I struggled to share too much with them. My secrets had piled up by the time I was a teenager. Any girl that found out too much about me would surely reject me, or that's what I thought. Better to be a boy with as little mystery and history as possible.

It was just one of a series of events that shaped me, most of them terrible on the face of it. But the coin always has two sides. The energy has to go somewhere, and for me it went into sports. And, although I couldn't see it at the time, it gave me a resilience and grit that my peers lacked. For them, sports was a fun little distraction. For me, it was a desperate escape.

CHAPTER 3

"Hi. I'm Tom, I'm the head instructor here."

"Hey, I'm Brenna."

Brenna leans down to shepherd a young boy along. She puts her hand on his lower back and ushers him forward.

"This, this is Kyle. I'm sorry, he's a little shy." Brenna unconsciously wipes a hair off Kyle's shirt as she talks, then does it again to make sure she got it off.

When you teach enough kids, you can tell instantly who wants to be there and who doesn't. Kyle doesn't really want to be here, but that's okay. I don't always want to be here, and I come anyway. Kyle is a clean-looking kid, so clean I wonder if his mother picked his clothes. What fifteen-year-old boy wears a polo shirt?

Maybe I'm just behind the times in fashion. I live most of my life in a gi or a rash guard, after all. I step forward and extend my hand to Kyle. "Hey, Kyle, how you doing, bud?"

He shows me a genuine smile and gives me his hand. His eyes look into mine, and his handshake isn't bad. His mouth opens to speak. "Hi, I'm—"

Brenna abruptly begins speaking over him. "He was looking at your school online, and I thought we could come by and—Kyle, ask him what martial art he does here."

Kyle looks at her with some embarrassment and says, "He does Brazilian jiu-jitsu, I told you."

"You look all this stuff—he looks all this stuff up." Brenna laughs for a few beats longer than normal and flashes a big smile. I feel as if

Kyle and I are already bonding over his mother, although I've know her all of ten seconds.

I go through our programs, what our academy offers, and so on. Everybody needs a different emphasis. Brenna, for example, doesn't need to hear about our world-class competition team. She needs to hear that her little boy will be safe and around good influences.

It goes well, and Brenna puts her deposit down. I fit Kyle for a gi, and everything is going well. Then Brenna says with a nervous laugh, "He won't be a little big for the kids in this class?"

"Oh, no, no, he'll be in the 6 p.m., with the adults."

She looks horrified, "Oh god no!" She gives another nervous laugh, "He's fourteen."

"Okay, so he should be in the adult class."

Brenna looks nervously at the class going on right now, which happens to be an adult class. There is a large range of people and body types on the mat, as always. But Brenna can only see the handful of my toughest guys. In her mind, everyone is a threat to her little boy.

"Will there be other children his age?"

"There won't be any children at all, including him."

"Will they be, like, doing this kind of stuff?" She motions to the mats, where some light sparring is happening.

"This is part of jiu-jitsu," I say gently.

She goes quiet, and I can tell I'm about to lose her. A quick glance at Kyle shows that I'm far from losing him. He watches the activity on the mats with interest. I see him ever so slightly leaning his body toward the students, like he's caught in a tide and it's slowly taking him out to sea. He's sold, but Brenna owns the checking account. I try a different approach.

"Hey, Kyle, how big are you, one-ten? One-twenty?"

He shrugs but gives a nod.

"You're not a big kid in your school, huh? Like some kids are as big as these guys, huh?" I motion to the class.

He opens his mouth but is swiftly cut off by his mother. "He's a little—"

"What was that, Kyle?" I say loudly.

Brenna chuckles uncomfortably. "Yes, Kyle, you tell him," she says, as if it was her idea.

He swallows and says, "Some are, but a lot of these people are bigger."

"Okay," I say, ready to make the hard sell. "So what if I promised you that if you come to class three times a week, in six months you'll have half of these people running scared from you?"

It's a stretch; jiu-jitsu progress doesn't come fast. But it doesn't matter. In six months, he may not be able to scare half the people in my academy, but he'll be able to scare everyone at his high school.

I step closer and put my arm around his shoulder. "Six months with us, size won't matter anymore."

I see Kyle's eyes change. He's off in some fantasy land now, effortlessly tossing his bully around the schoolyard. Brenna is watching, too. Something about my hand on his shoulder does it for her. The image of her son around some strong men for once leaves her without much to say.

"So the kid signed up?" my Dad asks.

"Oh, yeah," I say while slowly leaning back on the couch with satisfaction.

"No shit? You better make a man outta him now."

It's a few hours later and I'm at my parents' house enjoying a Saturday evening. Tom and Isabelle are running around the house, stopping in the living room where my parents and I sit and relax. My mother still has the energy to chase kids around. I usually do too, but I'm talking to my father tonight. We speak in quiet tones, occasionally raising our voices as a kid streaks through the living room.

I tell him about the teenager from earlier, and my father and I enter into a deep conversation about manhood and upbringing. He takes full credit for getting me into sports, something I don't quite remember the same way as him, but it's not worth arguing about. One thing we both agree on: sports very likely saved my life when I was young.

"Hell, you were doing shit when you were a teenager that was just crazy."

I shrugged and mumbled that it was a crazy time.

"Hell, you were getting tattoos in high school, son—and then there was *that* whole thing!" He points at my left arm. The scar faded over the years, but it would never go away. The warped skin still had the odd gleam from the burn mark.

When I don't say anything, my Dad says plainly, "Why'd you do that? Huh, son?"

I take a breath before replying. "Jesus took on all that pain, you know? Least I could do was feel just a little bit of that pain."

His face doesn't react at all, and he repeats the question:

"Why'd you do it?"

———————

Sports was always a big part of my life, not necessarily by choice. If it were up to me, I would have stayed home and watched the Muppet Babies. It was my mother who seemed hell-bent on enrolling me in every possible sports team. She never demanded that I win or cared if I lost. She just wanted to be a good mother, maybe give me some opportunities she never had. Maybe she also knew that I was restless, that I had too much spare energy. She may not have been aware of all of the fights I had been getting in with other kids, but she may have been more in the loop than I thought. Better to have me throwing balls downfield than bashing heads against concrete.

My parents came to almost all of my games, driving me all around the Northeast. Sometimes my father would show up half drunk or fully hung over, but he was usually there. My mother's trigeminal neuralgia wouldn't let up just because of an important game, and she was hit with waves of pain in the car and during my games. But she was also there. I didn't fully appreciate their sacrifice, but I knew that sport events made our unusual family feel normal. We weren't, of course. But we could pretend to be during those moments. Just another family cheering their son on.

I played everything, all year round. In the summer I was on the baseball field; in the spring I was on a basketball court. I had the signature DeBlass strength of my father and grandfather, but my real secret weapon was always my grit. I was a worker. My mother had crippling episodes with her trigeminal neuralgia, but she kept being a mom. My father suffered a terrible vertebrae injury and had to close down his own barber shop, but he kept being a dad. Resilience was in our blood. The last thing I was going to do was throw my hands up and quit because I was the runt on the block.

Which was no longer true, by the way. In middle school, my body started catching up to the rest of the kids. By the time I was twelve, I started to pull away from the pack. Little Tom wasn't the kid they threw rocks at in the sand pit anymore. I was rapidly approaching six feet. I was the only kid on the basketball team who could dunk. As my body got more coordinated, my grit that had carried me for so long became fused with my newfound physical strength. Suddenly I was kicking soccer balls that sent kids running for cover. I could hang off the rim in basketball. I was becoming an athlete, and Mom wasn't waking me up to go to practice on Saturday mornings any-more. Instead, I was the one running to her car after practice and negotiating for twenty more minutes so I could run a few more laps.

I played nearly every sport available through my schools, but in high school I settled into track and field as sort of my thing. There's a lot of politics in local sports; lots of stuff came down to who you knew on the school board or whatever. I was the best player on the basketball team, but I couldn't get played because the coach didn't know my parents. That bugged me enough that I started focusing on track. I liked the idea of competing against yourself. You beat your best time, or you didn't. There was no coach to blame or quarterback who didn't see you open downfield.

Track sports very much center around records and breaking them. I quickly learned that I loved breaking records. Once you break one, you want to break the rest of them. I had always loved jumping, so I took to the long jump. I mean, I really crushed it. I broke the county long jump record in middle school. By age thirteen or fourteen, I was jumping close to 20 feet. I broke the county record as a freshman and again as a sophomore in the long and the high jump.

I was an animal; I felt invincible. Most kids do at that age. I certainly hadn't learned the finer points of nutrition or hydration yet. I could shrug off injuries, and fatigue was something I had only heard about in stories.

My junior year, I fully expected to break the county record for a fourth time. I was running a 100-yard dash in 10.8 seconds, and I was on track for a 23-foot long jump. Instead, I tore my hamstring at a practice early in the year and was sidelined for the whole season. A hamstring injury is not serious, in the sense that you will inevitably recover. But it's still one of the most painful injuries an athlete can have. With a grade-three tear, you cannot walk without serious pain.

This may be a good time to talk about my relationship with pain. I had absorbed the pain of my parents for years. You can only put so much air in a tire, though. All of that energy needed to be released somehow. You're probably thinking that athletics was my outlet, the pure escapism of a complicated home life. But that's only half true. Put simply, I liked pain. I liked suffering. I wanted to experience it, and athletics was a way to get that. Maybe that's why I was so good at it early. When other kids would run until they got a cramp, I ran *with the hope* of getting a cramp. Then I would run harder to make it worse.

When I suffered my first serious injury during my junior year, I never once thought I was done. I woke up every morning and worked on rehabbing my leg. I didn't get depressed; in an odd way, it gave me a more intense focus.

I did eventually heal up and went back to playing basketball in the summer. During a practice, I was getting physical during an exchange. As I swiveled my body around an opponent, I felt a pop in my leg. Pops didn't scare me, and after doing a mental check for pain, I felt only a minor discomfort and kept playing.

ACL tears are like that; the pain sneaks up on you over the first few hours. By the end of the practice, walking back to the locker I felt my knee buckle and I stumbled. Twenty minutes later it happened again. The next morning, I knew something was wrong.

It was a full ACL tear at seventeen years old, coming off a grade-three hamstring tear. In sports, injuries happen. Everyone gets one for free. But after a second major injury in a short period of time, people look at you a little differently. There is a very real stereotype of the injury-prone athlete, the guy or girl who could have been great if not plagued with tears, sprains, and breaks. People started to look at me differently, especially coaches. I was supposed to be in my prime. Maybe in my mid-twenties, I could incur a major sports injury and still be "on track." But this was too soon.

I rejected all that bullshit. If I could rehab my hamstring, I could rehab my knee. My focus prior to my senior year shifted from breaking records to just getting back to healthy. Again my relationship with pain proved to be an asset. In seven months, I rehabbed my ACL just in time for the senior year of the track season. Senior year was already important, but it became even more important for me. It was my time to prove to everyone that injuries couldn't beat me, that my potential was still there. But it was also an important year for college scouts recruiting for talent. I wasn't a bad student, but I wasn't a great one either. If I'm being honest, I got by mainly on charm. I had a knack for making people like me, whether that was fellow students who could help me study or teachers who might go a little easier on me. It's not that I didn't work hard. I worked differently. I leaned on being social in school to be successful, something that is still underrated today.

But really, a track scholarship was the clear path for me to get to college. And even though no one in my family had ever graduated college, it wasn't an aspirational thing to me. Thanks to my mother, it was implanted in my brain from a young age that I was going to college. Period. There was no "if you work hard enough" or "if you choose to." It was "you're going." I was locally known as a track star, having broken the long jump record twice in high school. But with an injury and no record as a junior, I knew that colleges would weigh everything on my performance during the next few months as a senior.

That season, I jumped 23 feet and got offered a scholarship to Monmouth University.

If I'm painting a picture of a healthy young man, don't be fooled. The fighting that I mentioned before never stopped. I would regularly get in fights all through high school. I wasn't a bully. Bullies need to dominate weaker people to feel powerful. I was, oddly, the opposite. I would find myself in fistfights with people older, bigger, and stronger. When I was seventeen, I fought my first adult. The fight was broken up, but not before I got punched in the face. For some reason, I found him the next night and challenged him again. Thankfully he backed down. It probably wouldn't have gone my way. Around the same time, I fought another grown man at a house party and beat him up pretty good, even breaking one of my knuckles.

And when there were no sports to play or people to fight, sometimes I would just hurt myself. When I was sixteen I developed an obsession with Jesus and the crucifixion. This idea that one man could take so much pain and suffering for the world must have spoken to something deep inside of me. I heated up a metal coat hanger in the shape of a cross and branded it onto my shoulder. The pain was excruciating, but it was actually the smell that stuck with me. You expect it to hurt, but you don't expect the smell of burnt skin to be wafting around your room for the next hour.

Why did I do it all? I'm sure you can figure it out. I never tried to be my own psychiatrist. Healthy or not, the fact that pain was an ally of mine gave me an advantage as an athlete. Even then, the emergency switch in my brain that should have made me stop when things hurt was broken. And even when I was getting in those fights at seventeen, it scared people. When your opponent hits you, they need to see something in your eyes that registers your fear or your pain. My opponents didn't see that in my eyes. It was a powerful ally, one that would come in handy in the years to come.

CHAPTER 4

"Little badass, huh?" says my Dad with more than a little mocking in his tone.

"Yeah, you know how we are," I reply, referring to the DeBlass men in the family.

I'm just finishing telling him a little about me in high school. He listens, not stopping to ask many questions but nodding from time to time as if to check in and say he's paying attention.

I don't tell the story to my Dad as cleanly or as linear as I'm doing for you now. We fumble around a bit, dancing around certain topics. In theory, my father should know all of this. In reality, his memory is broken up by days or weeks of drug-fueled gaps where he was physically there but mentally lost in his addictions.

For my part, I don't stop and ask him what he remembers. I assume that he remembers nothing. My father plays along with this, never stopping to tell me that I don't have to explain something in particular.

We suddenly notice that the house has gone quiet. The kids are watching TV in the next room, and my mother has joined them now, silently watching and giving a father and his son some time alone. I stand and call to the kids that it's time to get home. I hug my mother, a warm prideful embrace. She loves me and she always has. When I hug my father, he pulls me a little tighter. He's always loved me too, but we both know there's been obstacles in the way. As we break and I get a look at his face, I see distress. I realise then that much of what I told was unknown to him and maybe a little upsetting. He knew about the fighting in my youth but maybe not about the pain that was behind it.

"You okay?" I ask quietly with my hands still on his shoulders. He nods right when tears well up. The kids come into the living room; there's no time to have the moment we might have otherwise had. Instead, I say, "We'll talk about it tomorrow."

He nods and turns his attention to bend down and hug the kids goodnight. They are oblivious to his mood. They are oblivious to his whole history, to any part of him that isn't their sweet, loving grandpa. More and more, I am starting to forget about the other side of him too.

I make a mental note to fast-forward to the good stuff next time we talk—the martial arts stuff.

Martial arts started for me in high school. Believe it or not, between playing every sport available, two major injuries, and everything at home, I actually did a little Taekwondo. As a combat sport, TDK is on the lower end of the violence spectrum. There are forms, technical drills, and limited-contact sparring. The sparring is very controlled; it emphasizes scoring clean hits. That's why it's often seen as a very "kid-friendly" martial art.

Like most kids, TKD was a fleeting thing for me. Once the major school sports like baseball and football open up, they tend to jump ship to play where the other kids are. But not surprisingly, I enjoyed hitting people, and I filed TKD away as something to come back to later.

I got my chance in college. After playing track and field for a while, I suffered another injury. This time I tore every ligament in my left leg. By now, injuries were a fact of life for me. I knew I would recover, I knew I would come back. But until then, why not try something different?

College was a strange time for me. I studied Education, getting my degree. It was a family milestone, no one else had graduated college. I was away from home, finding out more about myself. I wasn't like the other kids. I was a street kid, and I finally started to appreciate that. No one had seen the things I'd seen. I wasn't yet twenty-five, but I felt like an old man compared to them.

At the same time, I was still social in school. I got along with most people, continued to charm my teachers, went to parties, and had girlfriends. But in my own head, I was a loner. I was often pretending to be social; most people couldn't tell the difference. It troubled me sometimes how good I was at hiding myself from others. I was one hundred percent sober at this time. I didn't drink in college or for several years after. That's not easy to pull off in college, by the way. But growing up with my alcoholic father, I had developed a hatred for alcohol. My primary release from life was still pain, sports, and self-inflicted adversity.

One of the reasons combat sports are so popular in America is because after high school or college, a sports fanatic like me has limited options. Sure, there's always the local pickup games or maybe an amateur league. But I had a championship mentality. I played to win, to break records, to be the best. So I returned to a local Taekwondo school.

I am, in many ways, a TKD instructor's worst nightmare. I was a trained athlete, I was a psychotic competitor, and I liked getting hurt. I was a terrible fit for TKD. I was disqualified from tournaments for being too aggressive. I was the guy no one wanted to fight. I would blitz my opponents with a hundred punches in about three seconds. I treated it like any of the street fights I had been in all my life: come out swinging, and keep moving forward.

My form wasn't the cleanest, and I lost a fair amount of TKD matches because of this. The sport rewards clean, undisputed hits. This required a knowledge of range and timing. I was accustomed to taking one to give two. It infuriated me. If anything, the rules of the sport were the only thing saving most of these guys from me. And my coach at the time never seemed to fight for me. I was used to high-school coaches, who would get red in the face screaming at the referees for any perceived slight. It was just what a good coach did where I came from. The fact that my TKD instructors seemed uninterested in advocating for me when I was clearly the more aggressive fighter and athlete was hard to get past.

I needed to be unshackled, so after a short time in Taekwondo, I headed across town to Tong Dragon Mixed Martial Arts. Despite the name, this was my first modern MMA gym. Just the physical space fit me better. It was a large warehouse with plenty of mat space for grappling. There was a boxing ring in one corner and an MMA cage in the other. My attention was immediately drawn to both of them

I was pegged early on as a prospect for Tong Dragon. They could see that I was young, aggressive, and just naive enough to be dangerous. They steered me towards MMA right away, which was fine with me. I started off in the boxing and Muay Thai classes. I immediately felt everything I had been denied in TKD. I could spar with guys and really *connect* my punches, setting my feet and following through. When I did, none of my opponents at Tong's would crumple to the floor or give me a look of indignation. They would give it all back and more.

It was one of the first times in my life where the people were like me. They were tough; they had grit. Some of them weren't afraid of anything. Others were probably afraid of everything. Fighting wasn't "fun" for them. It was necessary. It was a piece of their mental health or maybe their mental dysfunction. But I wasn't judging. We all had some strange relationship with violence or pain, me as much as anyone. It was what drove us to come back to the gym.

And I did come back, night after night. I wasn't a prodigy; I didn't experience the thrill of victory for some time. I went home with bruises, cuts, strains, and wounded pride. But I didn't go to bed angry. I wouldn't go to bed at all. I would stay up all night, thinking and replaying the events of the last training session in my head. And I got angry—angry that I had been beaten yet again. I had to get back in the gym as soon as possible. I would drift through my day, present and yet somewhere else. Everything was a countdown to the moment when I would walk into that nondescript warehouse to see the harsh fluorescent lights, hear the blaring of gym music and a coach's voice booming over a class. Most days, I was literally looking forward to another beatdown, which tells you how much I loved it—or how psychotic I was. But it wasn't just the training. It was everything. The culture of fighting. Leaning against a wall between rounds. Wrapping hands while coaching someone in the ring. Cleaning the mats before leaving at night. I slowly fell in love with all of it.

I was home.

CHAPTER 5

"So you were good right from the beginning, huh?" says Dad.

I pause before my reply. "Naaw, I was . . . I had the talent, had the genetics and the stubbornness—"

"You're welcome."

I smirk but press on. "Like, in striking, you can walk in and be good. You can hit hard; you can be fast. You still need training to get better; you need a lot of it. But jiu jitsu is different. No one is good right off the bat. You can have *potential*, but you're not good."

My dad pauses for a few seconds, rubbing his chin with the palm of his hand before blurting out: "So you took that first fight with not a lot of experience, huh?"

I shake my head and smirk to myself. "Man, I had, like, zero."

"So why'd you do it?"

It's a fair question, and there's more than one answer.

"I dunno, I guess I was dumb, or maybe I was just not afraid enough. At some point you learn that you don't have to say yes to everything to prove you're not afraid."

My dad takes another pause for a block or two, working up the courage to ask his next question.

"So what happened?"

"You know what happened. You were there," I reply. I immediately feel guilty because I know what I forced him to acknowledge.

"I really don't, son. I was, uh . . ."

I cut him off. "It's okay. I forgot for a second."

He mumbles something dismissive and looks out the window in a kind of sulk. A moment of silence passes. There is still a solid fifteen minutes left in our drive. I decide to power through the moment. After all, there are too many of these moments in my story to stop and get hurt feelings each and every time. I remind myself that he wanted the stories for a reason. He was high or drunk or both for so much of my life. If he wasn't, he wouldn't be asking forty years later what the hell happened.

The moment of anger subsides, and I speak with a friendly tone. "Well . . . I learned a lot from that one. Let's just start there."

———

I loved hitting people. When you land a clean shot on someone, it's a feeling that you chase. Striking is intuitive; you hit the other guy without being hit. Of course, you quickly learn how difficult this is and that you will spend years of training just to put the fundamentals into play.

Still, striking was satisfying because it had regular payoffs. Even if you couldn't land a single jab in sparring, you could still work a heavy bag or some mitts.

I wanted to fight. I didn't care if it was MMA, boxing, or whatever. But MMA was the combat sport of the moment, and we were an MMA gym. I had decent hands at that point. I could throw with power, and I could take shots. I had yet to develop much in the way of footwork, range-finding, or tactics. But if you wanted to do MMA, eventually you would need to take a jiu-jitsu class.

Jiu-jitsu seemed complicated to me. Unlike striking, it wasn't very intuitive. I would watch pure BJJ matches, and I never had a real sense of who was winning or even what the objectives were. There was a purity to striking that I didn't see in jiu-jitsu, even though I respected the hell out of it. But I couldn't avoid grappling forever. If I ever wanted to do MMA, it would be required.

So I got onto the BJJ mats. Initially, I thought the one thing I would have going for me would be my strength. I was over two hundred pounds by now. I was lean, I lifted, I ate whatever I wanted. I would probably run through these scrawny little jiu-jitsu guys.

I remember rolling with a purple belt on my first day. He was probably a hundred and fifty pounds soaking wet. He looked like he should be playing World of Warcraft, not fighting grown men in a grappling match. In the opening seconds I ran him over like a garbage truck. I took him down with a football-style tackle. He wrapped his legs around me in guard, a position I knew about from watching MMA. I tripoded up to bear as much weight as possible on him, then set to squeezing him like a grape.

In the beginning I could tell he was thrown off by my pace, so it seemed like a good idea to just be intense and physical. I pinned him down and squeezed, but after a minute or so it became clear that I had no real idea how to tap him out. This kid just held onto me like a dead body. He didn't explode in an escape attempt. He barely even struggled.

He was in a totally different mindset. There was no urgency from him. When I ran out of ideas, I wondered if the match could be considered over. After all, I took him down and was on top. I had basically won, right? As the seconds ticked by, I started to get annoyed, then frustrated. Why wasn't this guy doing something? Did he want to win? After another minute of me trying to get him off of me, including picking him off the ground, he started to shift his hips around and make slow progress. My explosive movements had been dulled now. I was tired—and frustrated by the inaction. I barely noticed that my arm had been wedged between our bodies. I figured that it wasn't a real problem; I could yank it out at any time. But as the kid continued to squirm his way around me, he was now on my side instead of beneath me. I tried to stand again, but it was more awkward for some reason. I looked down to see he had somehow woven his skinny legs around one of mine. I lost my footing and returned to my knees. The kid kept moving and was now fully on my back. I thrashed around, making loud noises of effort and grunting. I was sweating, and I realized this annoying little purple belt was sneaking his arms around me. I grabbed his wrists with my giant, gorilla hands and tried to pull him away. But somehow my arm was now caught under one of his legs. I snorted in frustration with myself. It must have slipped under by mistake. Now I was fighting off his arms with just one of mine.

Eventually, the kid sank in a rear naked choke, which I stubbornly ignored. There was no way those skinny little arms were going to . . .

I snapped awake with a coach and some students looking over me and saying my name repeatedly to wake me up.

It was my first lesson about the power of jiu-jitsu. But it wasn't the one that made me fall in love with it. If anything, I thought of jiu-jitsu as annoying, like a series of tricks that would never work with striking involved. It was Taekwondo all over again. I thought I would have easily beaten that kid in an MMA match.

I kept training jiu-jitsu, though, because I had to. My focus was on basic defensive stuff. Sprawl and brawl, they called it. I didn't like it. I thought I was better at striking. Truthfully, I wasn't great at either. But striking has a way of lulling you into thinking you're better than you are. You memorize some combinations, learn how to circle and hit with more power. You hit things that don't hit back. Your coach says you're improving.

Jiu-jitsu is always done against a person who is probably doing everything to shut you down and beat you. It's harder to overestimate your jiu-jitsu skills, and I already didn't like losing. Still, I was training regularly in grappling. I might need it soon. My coaches at Tong's had arranged for a fight. As my first one, it was perfectly set up for me. The ruleset would be shooto boxing.

For those that don't remember or don't know, shooto boxing was a sort of precursor to MMA, although the two sports existed together for a time. In shooto there were no gloves, but you could only use "open hand strikes." There were also no elbows and no knees in most organizations. Other than that, it was an MMA fight. Matches would contain striking and grappling seamlessly. Most matches had rounds like MMA, and took place in a ring or octagon.

If it sounds like MMA with slapping instead of punching, that may be underselling it. Some of the legends of open hand striking, like Bas Rutten, could knock men out cold with slaps. This form of fighting has recently made a resurgence with the new "Combat Jiu-Jitsu" style of fighting.

It was a format slightly less dangerous than MMA with the omission of elbows and knees. I had also been matched up with an opponent who was also 0–0 like me. It was good fight, and I was training hard to be ready.

About a week before the match, my coaches took me aside and said they had some good news. They had "got me" an MMA fight instead, against another complete beginner making his debut. My coaches presented it like it was sort of absolute no-brainer. They said it would be better for my career, a better matchup for me. I asked if the fight was an amateur MMA fight. No, that's the best part, they said. It's a pro fight.

It wasn't. It was a pro fight in the sense that amateur fights had helmets and shin guards. We wouldn't have that. But MMA was still unsanctioned in New Jersey at the time. That meant not just elbows and knees would be allowed, but things that were normally illegal in sanctioned MMA, like knees to downed opponents or even soccer-kicking downed opponents.

It also was not a pro fight in the sense that it would not go on my permanent record—meaning I would gain literally nothing but my purse, which was a few hundred dollars. I wasn't crazy about being thrown into a Bloodsport-style match. But if the opponent was also debuting, maybe low stakes made sense.

He wasn't. Somehow my beginner opponent ended up being last year's "MMA Fighter of the Year" for the East Coast, a perfect 10–0 fighter. He could strike, he could grapple, and he could finish fights. He hailed from a known fight club. Hell, he had his own website. My whole gym didn't have one of those. I would be a lunch snack for him. I was confident, but not delusional. And yet I couldn't say no to the match. I knew I needed to, but the words just wouldn't come out of my mouth.

Sitting here now, an experienced coach myself, I would never allow a fighter I coach to take that match. My coaches knew it wasn't fair to me and it wasn't safe. There was an unsaid tension. I waited for them to tell me, *Hey man, you don't have to do this.* Or, even better, to tell me they weren't letting me do it. But it never came, and I never backed out.

In all fights, you have feelings of anxiety in the lead-up. Sometimes it's fear, real and justified. Other times it's irrational fear, just your body's chemical reaction to violence that's about to happen. It's often hard to tell which fear you're experiencing. This is especially true in your first fight. I had fought many times growing up. But MMA fights are different. For one, you have a hell of a lot more time to think about it. Weeks or months. That's not fun, especially when you know your opponent is, on paper, considerably better than you.

The other thing about fights is that there are always people around you trying to convince you you're going to win: coaches, training partners, friends. It's not easy to take someone aside and tell them they are the sacrificial lamb. It had never occurred to me that my coaches had their own conflict of interest. After all, they had a relationship with the promoter to protect. They had promised a fighter would be in the cage at the appointed time and place. It's not that they didn't care about me. But what was more important: their gym's reputation, or the guy that had been training for a couple months? Because of all these things, combined with my own naivete, when the night of my MMA debut came I actually thought that I had a chance. My hands were coming along; my defensive wrestling was getting there. I was aggressive and tough. Maybe this guy was sleeping on me. Maybe he had gotten lazy.

But then another feeling would come in, a more rational part of my brain that could do basic math. A 0–0 fighter with two months of training versus an undefeated veteran. Every few hours, these feelings of hopelessness and hope wrestled for control of my brain. Hopelessness won out most of the time.

To make matters way worse, most of my friends bought tickets to the fight, as well as people from my town that I barely knew. I had a reputation as a tough guy, even in the gym. Everyone knew I had potential. They just didn't realize that the potential hadn't got any time to grow. All they knew I was born to be a fighter. There was a lot of backslapping and "you're gonna destroy that guy" kind of talk. Every time it happened, I felt alone. Very few people knew what I was up against. People didn't just expect me to win—a lot of them thought I would win easily. I wasn't even sure if my coaches really understood; none of them had even fought in MMA before. Their experience was in shooto fighting.

I remember facing off against my opponent at the weigh-ins, seeing him for the first time. He struck me as emotionless. I couldn't read anything from him. He looked right through me, like I wasn't even a person. I was trying to hype myself up, to intimidate him. It was like trying to intimidate your computer when you play it in chess. I didn't know what to make of it. My gut told me that it wasn't good, but my brain and the brains (or at least the mouths) of my teammates told me that he was scared. I had fought a lot of men and looked into a lot of eyes by that point. I knew what fear looked like. He didn't seem scared to me.

The next night, I stood across from him in the cage. I remember the announcer introducing him as "having a perfect MMA record of ten wins and no losses." I think it truly hit me then. This was a professional, I was not. The gate was closing, and the various officials, announcers, ring girls, and cornermen were scurrying off. I saw and heard someone latch the cage shut with a definitive *clack!*

It was me, him, and the referee. The feeling of loneliness intensified and gave way to anger and rage. I have never been a good victim. When I get backed into a corner, I fight my way out. I was angry at myself, I was angry at my team, I was angry at everybody. You may think that this surge of anger was a good thing, that it would carry me past my normal limits in a fight, but that's not how real fights work. Emotional fighters make mistakes.

As soon as the match started, we closed the distance. I noticed right away that he was moving in a way I hadn't trained for. He was light on his feet, bobbing up and down, feigning, cutting angles. I tried to keep him in front of me long enough to set my feet and get some hard shots off. But he was moving too much. What's worse, he would hover in front of me just long enough where I would throw a punch or two. Finally, after a little range-finding, I moved to charge in and felt a crack on my nose as he timed a counterpunch on me. It was a clean shot and woke me up. I reacted to the blow by pressing forward again. I fired off a few more giant left and right hooks, which connected with nothing but air, and he danced backwards and around me. Each time I felt my hands not connect, I swung harder and extended my body a little farther. I was reaching more and more, then *crack!* A second punch to my nose, this one alarmingly loud. I felt woozy for a brief second before my focus came back. I looked up at the clock. About thirty seconds had passed.

I didn't charge forward again. I hadn't liked that last shot, and I was having trouble breathing through my nose already. My opponent read the signs immediately and turned it on. He pressed forward, leaning out of the way of a haymaker I was hoping to catch him with on the way in, and then shot off a one-two-three punch combination on me. I instinctively tried to backpedal, not circling away like I was supposed to. Real thinking had gone out the window. When the first seconds of a fight don't go the way you plan, it can often be very hard to stay mentally disciplined. As I backpedaled, I felt the metal of the cage suddenly on my back as I bounced into it, and it rebounded me straight towards a surging, undefeated fighter who smelled blood. *Uh oh,* I thought.

He timed it perfectly. A straight right against my oncoming head. It was like the difference between hitting a parked car versus a car moving straight at you. It stunned me down to the mat. As I automatically tried to rebound up, I was greeted with two or three head strikes that I couldn't even see. I blindly wrapped my arms around a leg and felt easily two hundred pounds press down on me as he sprawled me back down to the mat.

What happened next is blurry. There's only so much you remember taking shot after shot. He smelled blood in the water, and he knew what to do. I probably took about a dozen strikes to the head in about five seconds—all of them unanswered, as I was still processing the last one I took on the feet. I don't remember the referee stepping in, but he did. The fight lasted just a few minutes.

When a fight is over, we usually focus on the winner. We ask about their next fight or what they're doing to celebrate. We don't focus on the plight of the loser, because it's a depressing shitshow. Half your town and your parents showed up to see you get blasted, until the ref had to pull your opponent off your limp body to protect you. The night you spend in a hospital without health insurance, or the constant headaches you feel for months after. The winner gets a flood of phone calls and instant messages saying how great they did. The loser turns off his phone only to realize that he can't hide forever. Eventually he has to get back in the gym and see his friends and family again. Or maybe not. The loser sometimes wonders if he's any good at this fighting thing at all. Maybe he should just quit.

From my whole MMA debut experience, the thing I am most proud of is that I came back to the gym the next week. It wasn't easy. Most people didn't talk to me about the fight. They didn't know what to say. They couldn't even say it was a close fight, that I had at least looked good out there or I'd get him next time. The only thing they could have maybe said was that I was in a no-win situation. A debut MMA fight in an unsanctioned organization against an experienced opponent: nowadays, most athletic commissions wouldn't even allow that fight to happen.

But they couldn't even point that out, not within earshot of the coaches who put me in there to begin with. At the end of the day, I took the fight. I could have pulled out. I'm not hardwired that way, but I *could* have. Getting beat like that was enough to put anyone off of fighting. But it just made the chip on my shoulder that much bigger. I thought of my opponent, his fans, my friends, my coaches. I thought that one day I would get it all back. Because fuck them.

I thought of this every day for a long time. Then one day I met someone who would help me make it happen.

———•———

"I remember that one now. You were tore up about it for months."

I laugh. "I was tore up about it for *years*, Dad. Years. People from town talked shit to me about that for years."

"Really?"

"Hell, yeah. People would yell shit to me in bars back home, at the store, anywhere. You gotta remember, no one really respected fighters back then. It was the career of a fuckup. They thought I had gone into a fuckup career and I couldn't even do *that*. I would literally fight guys who said shit to me about that fight."

"Hey, you got in there and they didn't, though, huh?"

I grind my teeth just thinking about it. The car pulls to a halt and we sit in the parking lot. I should let him go in, but something inside me is wound up by the story.

"It's not enough," I say.

"What's not?"

I stare through the window, thinking about what it had been like to crawl back to Master Tong's and go back to training.

"Just getting in there. It's not enough. You go in there to win."

"Well, of course you want to win," he says.

"No, you don't *want* to. You have to. Because losing is the worst thing. It's so bad, it's . . ." I struggle to think of the word.

He finishes the thought. "Hateful."

I slowly nod my head as I try the word on in my mind. "Yeah, that's it, isn't it?"

"Yeah, I thought so." My father then leans across the seat, almost close enough to whisper, only he doesn't. What he says next is delivered in his normal voice, and it gives me a chill.

"I know about hate."

He abruptly turns and opens the car door, then gets out and shuffles to the clinic entrance. When he returns he's all smiles, like nothing happened. Maybe the methadone erased the last twenty minutes, or maybe it's an act. Either way, a part of me is glad for the reprieve. My father's words remind of things I'd rather never talk to him about—or anybody. You see, my father *does* know about hate. God and the Devil have raged inside him his whole life. God won out in the end. But, for a long time during my life, the Devil reigned.

CHAPTER 6

Maybe I should say some more things about my father: his duality, his toughness, his anguish. He had a hard life. His father was an alcoholic and he was growing up in a tough time and place. They're not excuses, but they *are* reasons.

Starting when I was in high school, he began to lay hands on me. My father was a legendary street fighter in Brunswick. One time he was wandering around town drunk as a skunk when three or four men jumped him, robbed him, and left him in a train station in his underwear. Days later, when my father recovered, he found them and beat each and every one half to death with a club.

I was maybe eighteen—a man in every way, but still growing into my own manhood. Parents have a power over their sons and daughters; they can make them feel like children well into adulthood. My father's alcoholism accelerated, possibly fueled by the deep truth settling in that I was separating my life from his. I would go on to be my own man, formed by all of the experiences of my childhood. For every sweet memory of my father there was another bitter one. It was like putting ginger in your drink: it only takes a little, and your whole drink tastes like ginger.

Perhaps my father thought there was always more time to make it right, to make up for lost time. But as it became clear that I was succeeding in college, thinking about getting credentialed to teach, and getting into martial arts, perhaps he feared that I would leave him—or, worse, have a disdain for him. There was also the fact that I was beginning to study martial arts, becoming skilled as his body began the long but inevitable process of breaking down due to age, a process accelerated by his recklessness with substances.

As this happened, my father became more aggressive when he drank. I would spend most of my time away from home. When I would return, he would be brooding on a couch, as if he had been thinking about what he would say and do to me over the course of the night's drinking. He would get in my face, inches away, try and provoke me. He would call me a coward, a cunt, and a pussy. I never hit him, I never lost it. Until I did.

I had bought two kittens. I've always loved animals. They had health issues. They were fragile and sickly. It made my bond with them even greater. Ever the protector, I found time to take them to the veterinarian every day for their medicine. It was an hour drive. In return, they loved me unconditionally, more like dogs than cats.

I had returned home from the vet's office, noticing and ignoring my Dad's dark eyes this evening. I knelt to take them out of their crate, moving slowly so that they wouldn't get scared. I picked up one, and then the other, and cradled them in my arms.

I don't know what it was, and I guess it doesn't matter, but my father went into a rage. He stood up and bounded across the room, I thought he would tackle me. He stopped just short, his sweaty face taking up my entire field of vision and his alcohol breath filling my nostrils. He shouted at me, terrible things to say to any person. But I wasn't any person, I was his child.

I was taller than my Dad now, and bigger. But he had caught me in a kneeling position, a kitten in both arms. The cats recoiled in fear, burying their heads into my armpits. They were too small to leap out of my arms and run under the nearest couch.

I cradled them both and tried to cover their ears. I did my best to ignore my father, whispering, "Shhhh . . ." to the kittens while feeling the spit from his mouth hit my face. He called me a cunt, a loser, a pussy, and a coward. Anything he could. The kittens moaned softly in my arms.

I don't remember setting the kittens down, but I must have. I only remember lunging at my Dad. He got in a punch that might have dropped me a few years earlier. But not today. I shrugged it off and saw the look on his face change from a sort of satisfaction to concern for himself. I tackled him onto the couch, practically breaking the old thing into pieces. Cushions fell off and the window blinds crinkled from the kinetic force of two grown men fighting on a cheap garage-sale couch. I pressed his face down into the cushions and wrapped my hands around him. The veins in my arm bulged, and other veins in his head bulged. His face went red as his body struggled to muster up all the energy he needed on short notice while under the debilitating effect of drugs. He gripped my wrists with his hands, the same hands I had seen him break bricks with as a child. But against all my rage and power, he could not move me in the slightest. He looked into my eyes, and I into his. I saw real fear in his eyes, maybe for the first time ever. He knew that he was completely at my mercy and that he had given me very few reasons to have any in the past few years.

Thankfully, strangling someone with your bare hands takes several minutes, which was enough time for me to release my grip and come to my senses. We stared at each other for a moment in silence, each of us heaving big breaths. In that moment, the balance of power in the house shifted forever. I knew that my father would never touch me again for fear that I could kill him.

I scooped up my cats and brought them upstairs, leaving him brooding on the corner of his couch in a half-destroyed living room.

CHAPTER 7

"Don't do that."

The kid looks up at me, trying to get his breathing under control. "What?"

"You don't need to roll that hard with him. Just let him work."

The kid, one of my hotshot blue belts, looks indignant but doesn't say anything. The two return to rolling, but this time the new student is getting a generous amount of coaching from his partner.

I walk away. It's not exactly what I meant, but it's better than what they were doing. Rolling light doesn't mean coaching. When you stop to coach someone, you're not letting them experience sparring. But it's okay. This blue belt is in a selfish time in his training. He's twenty-something, hardwired to kill. I can't win the battle against his hormones in one talk, but maybe I can win a war of attrition over time.

After class, he approaches me. "Coach, I'm sorry about that."

I wait to see what kind of apology I'm getting, but he leaves it at that simple statement. Again, I'll take what I can get for now. One day, he'll say what he's sorry *for doing*, to show me that he understands what the problem was. You can't roll as hard as you want with an inexperienced student.

I put my hand on his shoulder to reassure him. "For sure. Just go easy, killer. You want these guys to come back, huh?"

He pushes back: "Hey, iron sharpens iron, though, right?"

"It does, but maybe he doesn't want to be sharpened right now. Maybe he's not even sure if this is for him yet."

"You're right, you're right. I'm just trying to push myself."

He turns to walk away, but I'm not sure if he really heard me, so I stop him.

"Okay, well, let's push you."

He turns and his face brightens. "Yeah?"

He thinks I'm going to invite him to some secret class, or to roll with me, or maybe even promote him. He's about to be disappointed.

"I want you to roll with him every class now. Every class at least once. And I want you to let him tap you every time."

He laughs it off nervously, but I double down, "I'm serious. Every time. And he can never know. You can't let him know you're giving it to him."

He says something; I'm not sure how to take it. "Is that how you got good with Ricardo?"

"Ricardo and Kurt beat my fucking ass every night. But that's because I was one of them, or least I wanted to be. They would never do that with someone that didn't want that. You understand what I'm saying."

He looks down, "Yeah I get it. He's not there yet."

"Right!" I say emphatically, nodding my head. "See, you get it."

He nods as well, and for that moment the lesson is over. I'm too busy to watch this kid every night and see if he will follow my instructions. But I make a mental note to follow up. Losing humbles you, but losing on purpose so that someone else can learn humbles you more.

It's certainly not a lesson I learned from Kurt.

———•———

A girl at my gym introduced me to a friend of hers. She told me that he was training for the highest levels and needed tough training partners. Back then, MMA was scarce enough that a "working fighter" would often take matches in shooto, Pancrase, or any promotion that would pay. His name was Kurt Pellegrino, and he was the first serious jiu-jitsu fighter I ever trained with.

This was in the mid-2000s. Jiu-jitsu was more popular than ever, but there were still very few American black belts. Brown and purple belts were seen as godlike in a town starved for good training partners.

After my loss in MMA, I returned to training with a vengeance. I was fueled by the hatred of losing and humiliation. Revenge is a powerful reason to get out of bed. Every person that laughed at me, every sideways comment, every pitying look went in a mental ledger.

I had been training jiu-jitsu for awhile, with a big emphasis on defensive jiu-jitsu. I had a basic jiu-jitsu survival kit for MMA: shrimp escapes, hitting my knees, maybe a guillotine or an armbar. But I still saw BJJ as a necessary evil.

Kurt changed all that. I had seen plenty of guys slow me down and annoy me with jiu-jitsu. Kurt was the first guy who showed me the offensive power of the art. He could do it all: his wrestling was strong, his striking was sharp. But when it came time, he would always put you away with a submission. I finally saw how powerful jiu-jitsu could be in the hands of a well-rounded athlete.

But Kurt's secret weapon was his toughness. Kurt was like me; he could out-train anyone. And he did—that was the problem. He needed training partners that could keep up with him. What I lacked in skill, I made up for in grit and athleticism. Kurt didn't need a BJJ black belt to spar with. He needed someone who could go ten five-minute rounds six days a week.

Through Kurt, I began to see jiu-jitsu as a sort of universal currency. It was usable in everything, from MMA to sambo or even street fights. A jiu-jitsu fighter could always find work, especially if he had a black belt. There was a mystique back then about the black belt. It still commanded a healthy respect, if not fear, to an opponent who hadn't trained in ground fighting.

Tough guys are hard to find, and even if I wasn't tapping many people out, I was making everyone work for it. It was my first truly marketable skill. Everyone could use a durable training partner. Because of this I was invited to train with Kurt's teacher, Ricardo

Almeida. Ricardo was a jiu-jitsu black belt. There was a mystique about him. For one, he had already fought in the UFC and was turning his attention to the King of Pancrase promotion in Japan. Also, he was the first Brazilian I had ever met. Ricardo did not live up to the stereotype of the easygoing Brazilian. I remember he was serious, intense. He was Renzo Gracie's first black belt, and it's not an exaggeration to call him one of the top fighters in the world at the time. He was where Kurt wanted to be, where all of us wanted to be. Daily training with Kurt led me to weekly training with Ricardo. Ricardo had his own stable of fighters, exposing me to a whole new group. Unlike Master Tong's team, these guys were all deadly serious about the world of MMA and jiu-jitsu. They treated training like a job even though none of us, save for Ricardo, was making a living off of it. Yet.

With Ricardo and Kurt, I began learning about the science of fighting. More than techniques, it was also tactics: cage positioning, ring control, wall wrestling, and the various meta-rules of MMA. Of course we mainly just fought a lot, but for the high-level guys, any edge was worth having. Knowing about scoring that takedown in the final seconds of a round could be the difference between show-money and win-money.

I remember the first time I sparred with Ricardo, he beat my ass. Even more so than Kurt, Ricardo had a maturity to his jiu-jitsu. They called him "Big Dog," and he was. And the most impressive part of that title was the group of men he was considered the big dog of.

My jiu-jitsu also continued to develop. I became difficult to submit and almost impossible by anyone other than Kurt, Ricardo, or a few others. Taking someone down and controlling them began to feel more natural, and even preferable. In MMA, jiu-jitsu had a direction, a purpose. Takedown, top position, attack. It was a good framework for learning, even though there was so much more to it. Eventually I received my blue belt. The blue belt is the moment you feel like you're "in" with the rest of the team, recognized as not merely the new guy anymore. It's the belt that makes you feel like you belong, and I did.

I was tied in deep enough with the team that I was invited to travel to Japan to corner Kurt as well as two other Renzo students: Joe D'Arce and Fabio Leopoldo. I was only a blue belt at the time, but again, I had toughness and grit. Just being a warm body that would actually come back and train after a day of beatings made you in a minority.

I remember showing up to the airport for the flight out to Japan. Eager to impress, I was the first one there and claimed a large area that would be "the Gracie gate" at the terminal. A contingent of Renzo students would be flying together.I borrowed my girlfriend's Game Boy to pass the time on the sixteen hour flight. It was bright pink. I sat in the airport, idly fiddling with it.

"A pink Game Bahoy! What is this ghuy, a gay?" said a booming voice behind me.

It happened so fast I didn't really process the thick Brazilian accent that strung every word as one long sentence. I just stood up, ready to beat the shit out of whoever said it.

"Listen, asshole . . ." I began as I turned. I cut myself short when I saw the grinning face of Renzo Gracie. He had a wild look in his eye, what I later learned was his default look. It could have been a tense way to meet, but Renzo flowed into the next moment in a way that relieved any tension. He cackled at his own joke and slapped his hand on my shoulder. He was in my personal space in half a second, shaking me like I was his nephew. I was pretty sure he had no idea who I was, just picking me out by my Ricardo Almeida t-shirt. But he was happy, almost too happy, to see me. I would go on to learn that Renzo had a magnetism to him. He picked people from their orbit and brought them into his as he passed by. It was one of his many talents. He and I were friends instantly. Then again, Renzo does that with everyone.

Little did I know that from the moment Ricardo decided that he liked me and was going to keep inviting me to his New Jersey academy, I had thrown in with a team. Ricardo was part of a small, tight-knit group of fighters all affiliated with Ricardo's teacher, Renzo Gracie. In addition to regular training with Kurt, I was going to Ricardo's once a week to train, and all of us would often go the Renzo Gracie Academy in New York. Renzo Gracie was the grandson of Carlos Gracie, a founding father of Brazilian jiu-jitsu. While many of the Gracie family left Brazil to settle in California, Renzo planted his flag in New York. With little in the way of competition, the Renzo Gracie Academy became the most prominent jiu-jitsu school in New York, and it is today thought to be the largest academy in the United States in terms of student enrollment (there's some debate on this, but it's definitely in the top tier).

But in those days the team was small, because we lived by the law of the jungle: only the strong survived. The mats at Renzo's had a murderers' row of training "partners," guys that made Kurt seem like junior varsity and me seem like pee wee.

There were Renzo's two brothers: Ryan and Ralph Gracie. Both were savage fighters who couldn't have been any more different in disposition from Renzo. They were both rough characters who liked to fight and would do so at the drop of a hat if you disrespected them or their families.

There was Renzo's cousin, Roger Gracie, a quiet, somewhat unassuming man who was already being called "King Roger" in the gym. He had won both ADCC and the IBJJF Worlds already, something most people spent their whole careers working towards. He would go on to win the Worlds several more times and even fight in the UFC and Bellator. Rolling with Roger was like that scene in Star Wars where everyone is trapped in a trash compactor, slowly crushing them to death. Roger didn't do anything fast, but he would slowly and methodically take your options away. He was known as the patient Gracie. I never saw anyone submit him, and I never saw him lose his cool. Roger would often show up with a hot prospect in the world of jiu-jitsu, Braulio Estima. Back then, he was just a really good kid who had potential. He would go on to be another world-beater, even having a technique named after him (the Estima Lock).

Kurt and I had some insane sparring sessions. Striking, wrestling, jiu-jitsu—he was better than me in all areas of fighting. But I might have been his equal in stubbornness and resilience. I would receive many ass-kickings from Kurt over the next few years. But I also was never completely outclassed by him, even in those early days. I was always in the fight, even if just by sheer grit. And, slowly but surely, my striking began to improve and my jiu-jitsu got smoother. I was matching my heart with a little skill now, and the training sessions with Kurt and the rest of his team got more manageable.

At the same time, my confidence increased. Every time I saw Kurt take a fight, he would dominate. The man was unstoppable back then. And every victory for him was a victory for me, because I knew that if Kurt could win, I could win—because I was giving Kurt tough rounds back home. The peak of this vicarious living was when our team went to Japan to corner Kurt for the 2004 King of Pancrase tournament.

Pancrase was a variant of MMA, taking place in a ring and allowing for strikes and grappling. In 2004, it had incorporated virtually the same rules as American MMA. That night, Kurt fought a Japanese fighter named Satoru Kitaoka. I remember watching Kurt work like a true martial artist. He shot for a single leg and transitioned to a suplex when Satoru tried to guillotine. When Satoru tried to work a guard, Kurt took his back. When Satoru tried to stand up for a slam, Kurt transitioned to mount. He was two steps ahead the whole match. Or, at least, until he wasn't. Fortunes can change fast in a fight, and Satoru managed to sink in a guillotine early in the second round and tap Kurt out. It was a bad way to lose a match, tapping out to a hail-mary choke to an opponent you were dominating. It was the highest level opponent I had seen Kurt fight so far, and it got me thinking that if he could compete at that level, so could I.

I started thinking about fighting again. I was leagues better than I had been since my first fight. Training with Kurt, but also his whole team, had accelerated my learning. I was picking up more that I ever would have at Tong Dragon in a fraction of the time. This time, I would do it the right way. I could compete in an amateur MMA fight, which was much more appropriate for me. At the same time, I was training with pro-level fighters. Kurt was already in talks to debut in a promotion called World Extreme Cagefighting (WEC), which was known for being a feeder league for the UFC. We could all see where his career was going.

CHAPTER 8

"So this was about the time that Isabelle came?" says my father. We're on the highway, driving again to the clinic. I relate to him, with a little less clarity, the story of my early days training with Team Ricardo Almeida. Some parts, like the intricacies of the Gracie family, I gloss over for his sake.

From time to time my father will interrupt me with questions, often just as I think he is losing interest. He will glance out the window silently until I wonder if I've lost him. But so far, he is hanging in there.

"Yeah, I guess. I was twenty-seven, so right before my first MMA fight."

My father grins. "Wild man got tamed, huh?"

Images of me staying up all night, going to strip clubs, and drinking too much pop up in my head. I decide to keep them private. My dad knows more than he lets on anyways. All of that largely stopped after Isabell. You go from the guy corralling people to go out for drinks after training to the guy saying that he has to get home.

"You don't know the half of it." I chuckle to myself.

"Oh, I bet I know some."

We drive awkwardly for a few seconds before I blurt out, "She gave me a reason to live, you know."

It's not meant as a shot at my father or his parenting, but I realize there's not many other ways to take it. He says nothing. I know I shouldn't go on, but I do. "Before Isabelle, I honestly didn't care if I lived or died. Sometimes . . ." My voice trails off.

But my father knows what I'm going to say and says softly, "You thought dying wouldn't be so bad."

His voice has a strange mix of shame and certainty. I search for the words to reassure him.

"It wasn't because of you or Mom. You were great parents. I just felt . . . lost. That's all."

He raises his hand to stop me. "I know. You don't have to explain."

It's not the first time I've wondered if I saved my father's life simply by being born.

———◆———

It was around this time that I started trying to date—at least, date more intentionally. Truth is, I could always meet girls. But as I got a little older, a feeling set in that I wasn't meeting the right girls, the "mother of my children" type. I joined an online dating site. You know the one that matches you based on your personality? Maybe that's every dating site. I was an MMA fighter, a Brazilian Jiu-Jitsu guy, and a gym rat from Jersey.

But in most ways, all of those things just scared the good ones away. I thought maybe online dating would even the playing field. It's also worth noting that I wasn't famous and my profession was not mainstream. I had to work just as hard as any other guy, maybe harder, to find a sweet all-American girl.

It didn't take long. I mean, it *really* didn't take long. I met a girl in just a few weeks. We went on a blind date, presenting a nice, sanitized picture of ourselves and our lives to each other. She was kindhearted, beautiful, and interested in me. The chemistry was there. Every date was different; we were always on our best behavior. At the end of the night, or the next morning, we would go back to our lives. She knew I was into martial arts, I knew about her job and her hobbies. But we hardly knew the *real* us. And that was okay. We had time. Plenty of time.

She was pregnant within the first year.

It was one of those things that, the moment we found out, we knew we were screwed. When we saw the lines on the stick, we looked at each other almost as if for the first time. We searched each other's eyes and saw the mixture of elation and terror. Rather than letting our pretenses slowly exit the stage for the real people behind them to step forward, our relationship had to mature at a breakneck speed. We had to get health insurance, meet parents, move into my place, and buy a hundred items for a baby. And we had to do it all right now. It was a stress test no two-month relationship could survive.

I knew things would be different when Isabelle was born, but like most parents you underestimate just how much your life as you know it is over. The thing with kids is that they never stop. There's no breaks. You're on their schedule. When they need you, you stop what you're doing to be there. And not just a little bit there. It's one hundred percent. I used to think that I could just have my kids around while I train or teach. Like they would just be quietly playing in the background. It doesn't work that way for at least a few years. Kids, especially babies, need to attach to their parents. They need to be loved, soothed, and looked after. And if you don't do that, they will make your life a living hell in that moment and in the long term. It's that simple.

In competitive sports, you see a fair amount of absent parents. Guys are so dedicated to the sport, to their goals, that children become an inconvenience. Their goals become largely about keeping their children occupied so that they can train.

I made a commitment to be with my kids as much as possible. But, as my mother always said, you still have to work no matter what. My career was competing and running my school. It wasn't just a dream, it was my livelihood. Luckily, martial arts is largely a night gig. So when my kids went down for sleep, I was jumping in my car and headed down for a long night of training.

My lifelong affinity for suffering and hardship took a new turn. Suddenly, I was suffering *for* something: my little girl, and eventually my son, Thomas.

I was married shortly after Isabelle was born. Delilah was and is a private person. As I became a known person in the world of BJJ and MMA, I did what I could to keep her out of it and let her live a private life. I still do.

She is the best mother my children could ask for. She would probably say something similar about me. Our relationship as parents survived, even if our relationship as husband and wife did not. Being parents isn't romantic. On top of that, everyone changes from their twenties to their thirties, often into totally different people. That's what happened with us. We became different people. It's no one's fault. It's just life.

This didn't happen immediately. In fact, we would have one more child together, Thomas. We loved them both with all our hearts. It was important that they grow up in a household with their parents. So we set aside our differences and our marriage and lived in the same house together. We never fought in front of the kids. They always saw us as their parents and still do. We are one hundred percent committed to co-parenting. We show up at their games and dance recitals; we are always together on the holidays. They will remember us as being a unit, just as I saw my mother and father. When the time comes, we will tell them. I fear that it will come sooner than we'd like. I can only hope we will do the best we can for them until then.

It wasn't easy to live like this, but it was familiar in a way. My mother's and father's marriage had its ups and downs. If I'm being honest, it was probably hanging by a thread behind closed doors over the years. My mother, in particular, sacrificed, and I had the idea of what it took. She lived with an addict through the worst times of his life. For me, living with the mother of my children, who was essentially a good person, didn't seem nearly as hard.

In this new arrangement, all my spare energy went into training, fighting, and winning. And the wins were about to start coming.

CHAPTER 9

I sit on the easy chair in the living room of my parents' house, the same house I grew up in. They've made a lot of changes over the years. Sometimes I forget that this was the room where my mother and I would literally pick my Dad up off the floor and get him on the couch after a particularly bad bender. But there are plenty of good memories, and that's what I tend to latch onto.

I feel comfortable here, and my kids love it. My son runs around half naked like the crazed kid that he is. If he could climb the roof to howl at the moon, he would. Isabelle cuddles up to her grandmother on the couch. In the next room I hear the clink of dishes and running water as my Dad cleans up after a family dinner.

It's a kind of song of the house. A busy house filled with people and love. The blare of the TV, and heavy footfalls of Thomas in the next room. The soft voice of my mother saying something to Isabelle that makes her giggle. Running water and suds in the kitchen. And . . .

I frown as I try to place the missing instrument in the song on the house. I mentally account for everyone in the household until I realise that I no longer hear the sound of plates being stacked and other ones being scrubbed clean. I lean forward from my comfortable chair to peek into the kitchen. My dad is standing at the kitchen sink. His silhouette is never quite upright; it slants and slopes as if a giant foot stepped on my Dad and we could never quite straighten him out again.

In many ways, that's metaphorically what happened. Years of hard work, injuries, and drug abuse have left him virtually crippled. Traversing the house, the street, and a vehicle is doable, but hiking or anything athletic is out of the question.

His head is low and his slouch is pronounced. I see his eyelids shut. The water continues to run and the soap gradually rises from the sink. The steam from the hot water is visible under the kitchen light, no doubt fogging up his glasses.

I stare at him for a second, then begin to count to ten in my head. When I get to six, his head rises and his hands resume the motions of dishwashing. He doesn't look over his shoulder in embarrassment, or to see if anyone saw what just transpired. In fact, It's like it didn't happen, and to him it probably didn't.

"Fucking methadone," I say to myself with a nervous relief.

The song of the house resumes. All is well. I text a friend about the incident, recognizing the humor of the old man nodding off during dishwashing. Dad cheerfully scolds Thomas for running through the kitchen, and I think I hear him hum a tune quietly.

Later than night, I lie in bed thinking about him. I am less confident in the humor of the situation now. Dad takes methadone every morning. Not every evening. I've seen him out of it before, but this feels off to me. Something doesn't add up.

———•◆•———

In just under a year with the Renzo Gracie team, I had fallen in love with grappling. I still liked hitting people, of course. But jiu-jitsu had a special appeal. It was the techniques, the physicality, the fact that you could do it with full speed and power. It was hard to box with full speed and power for very long. I also saw that grapplers were winning fights, especially at that time. You were far more likely to get away with limited striking than with limited grappling. The Renzo Gracie Team was destroying everyone with jiu-jitsu. Kurt and his teacher, Ricardo, were both fighting in Pancrase. Ricardo had won the King of Pancrase middleweight title. Ryan Gracie was fighting in Pride FC, and his student, Fabio Leopoldo, was the IFL middleweight champion.

There was definitely a focus on MMA at the team. But the world of grappling had its own rewards. Jiu-jitsu tournaments were growing in popularity. At times, I drastically underestimated how good I was getting at grappling. On the mats with people like Roger Gracie, I felt outgunned. We didn't have many casual jiu-jitsu athletes to compare myself to. But I wanted to compare myself to others in jiu-jitsu.

And yet, the sting of my first MMA fight had never gone away. They say the best competitors hate losing more than they like winning, and that was definitely me. I hated everything about that fight: not just losing, but being there with no experience, no fight camp. I knew that, before I started my pro jiu-jitsu career, I had to revisit that chapter of my life. I needed to return to the cage and get that win back.

I did it the right way this time. I got an amateur MMA fight against an opponent who had similar experience to myself (not zero, but not 10–0). Being part of a very reputable team helped here. Ricardo and Renzo had a healthy stable of fighters, and promoters wanted to feature them on their cards. They knew a Renzo Gracie student would show up, make weight, and probably bring an audience with them. In the lead-up to the fight, I remember the team around me knowing exactly what I was going to experience. All of them had pro fights—in fact, my amateur fight was almost trivial in a gym like that. It's not that it didn't matter; it was just expected that I would win. We were a team that won. It wasn't arrogance. Our records spoke for themselves. We won because we trained harder and had the best fighters. Very few teams in the world had as many pro fighters under one roof as ours. I fought them every day, and on some days I could get the better of them. The fear that I had felt before my first fight wasn't there. No one I could fight was scarier than Renzo's brothers or cousins, or Kurt and Ricardo.

I knew I was doing it the right way because, as the fight got closer, I was looking forward to representing my team and showing off my jiu-jitsu. My opponent was the one that should be scared.

It was a strange role reversal the evening of the fight. Now, I was the confident one, not displaying much in the way of emotions. I had picked up a sense of professionalism from Ricardo and the team. This was their job, their craft. It's not that the energy wasn't real: my body was electric. I felt the crowd, my coaches, the smell of the mats, and the heat from the announcer. But unlike last time, I didn't feel like I needed to be angry. It was the opposite. I had become a tactical fighter, one who would need all his wits in the next fifteen minutes.

In the opening minutes of the fight, I circled the ring, felt for my range, and probed my opponent. I was feeling him out, how disciplined he was, how reactive he would be. After half a round, I realized I was fighting myself. Not that he was some mirror image of my skills and techniques. He was Tom from years ago. He was Tom from my first fight. He was tough, and he had training—more training than Tom had in his first fight. But I was better, and I knew it. So did he. Every small movement I made provoked a reaction from him. He was on a hair trigger, overthinking my every move. He saw traps in every motion.

After some more setups, I pulled the trigger. I shot in, took him down, and started working the classic Renzo Gracie top game. At some point a scramble ensued, and I snatched up a leg. I cycled through some attacks as he flailed, trying to escape. I ultimately locked in a toe hold, a rare submission even today in MMA, let alone in the mid-2000s.

The win felt great. My whole town wasn't at this one. There were far less family and friends. It was Ricardo and some other close training partners. The people that mattered were there. I felt happy, but more so relieved. It was done, and so was I. From the moment my hand was raised, I knew I never wanted to fight in MMA again. I could be happy with just this one win.

Oh, how wrong I was.

CHAPTER 10

He's a young kid—twenty-four years old, I think. MMA fighter, still young in his career. Two wins and no losses. We take turns doing mitt work for each other. After every class, I work striking with the team at Ocean County. We do a little bit of everything: heavy bag, mitts, cardio, combinations, and power punching. Believe it or not, I have always felt more comfortable striking than grappling when it comes to MMA.

I am always the most tired at this point in the evening, hours into our class schedule, after I've not only taught a class but also run a full sparring session, which can go for an hour on some nights. Tonight, the kid puts me through the paces. At thirty-eight, I'm a young man by most standards. In the world of grappling, I'm middle-aged. In the world of MMA, I'm old.

Of course, I'm in better shape than ninety-nine percent of men my age, and maybe ninety-five percent of people in general. I diet, I lift weights, and I train daily. But the problem is that so does everyone else.

As I square up with the kid, he dances around with jerky movements and theatrical feints. He is a sound MMA fighter, but maybe he's a little preoccupied with showing off to any potential onlookers. I came up at Ricardo Almeida's school, where there were no onlookers. We also basically went full contact in training; we don't do that at my school. We train for technique, not to put each other out night after night. So I let him do his thing and I simply look for angles and slip punches, and keep him at range with jabs. The kid is mostly a good sport, matching his speed with mine but occasionally unleashing a flurry of punches just to show that he can.

And you know what? *He can.* He doesn't outclass me; I mostly brush aside his various hooks and jabs. But as I study his movements, I have to admit that his natural attributes are impressive. He's fast and he's young. He doesn't get tired, and he has that all-important killer instinct. He will be a formidable fighter in just a few years.

It makes me think about my unnamed, faceless opponent in ONE FC. I would like to fight a veteran, someone from my era with my experience—an interesting fighter, and an exciting fight. I'd like to think it's in ONE's interest to give me that kind of fighter, and I believe that they will.

But they don't have to.

The timer rings, and the kid takes off his gloves and immediately goes to the cardio station to keep working. He's been here since 6:30 training. It's almost ten in the evening. He's 2–0 professionally, but I can't see ONE FC putting me against anyone so inexperienced. They will send an experienced fighter with a winning record. Someone who wants to beat Tom DeBlass, who can make big moves in their career off a name like that. They will have everything to gain and little to lose. I know firsthand the reckless freedom that comes from being underestimated. It was once one of my most powerful tools.

———•———

You may or may not know what ADCC is, so I'll try and describe it. It's arguably the most prestigious grappling tournament in the world. It's far more arguable now, but in the 2000s there was no real debate. The best fighters in the world fight in many promotions. But ADCC is special for a few reasons.

For one, you cannot just sign up. You need to either be invited or win the trials. The ADCC organizers invite the top grapplers in the world. And I do mean the world. There is always an international flair to the event, as not just Brazilians and Americans show up. Athletes from Asia, Europe, and the Middle East are always present, even if just to make sure there is a healthy geographic representation. This gives the event a feeling akin to the Olympics, as fans may be rooting for their country's hero. That, combined with the every-other-year schedule, rounds out the Olympic feel.

But ADCC wants to allow breakthrough talent to surprise fans. They want to discover the next great grappler as well as showcase the top ones. That's why they reserve a number of slots at the world championships for "trials winners."

The idea is that tournaments will be held all over the world for one year. The tournaments will each have one winner (well, one for each weight class), and they will be allowed to fight in the ADCC Championship in the next year alongside all the invitees.

Winning the ADCC trials is considered one of the most significant accomplishments in grappling. You must emerge victorious in a tournament with anywhere from thirty to even more than sixty competitors, often resulting in more than ten fights in a single day. It's big enough that just winning the trials can turn you into a star (at least in the grappling world), regardless of how you perform in the championship. Trials winners have a rich history of medaling and even winning the championship, often winners completely unknown to the grappling world. Former winners include Marcelo Garcia, Eddie Bravo, Craig Jones, and Lachlan Giles.

ADCC was a part of the Renzo Gracie team culture.. Renzo himself was close to the ADCC organizers, the Royal Family of the United Arab Emirates. Renzo would *always* have his team training for ADCC trials; they were the de facto Gracie family team for many years and still are.

But there was yet another angle that made ADCC special: ADCC winners had a habit of getting noticed, and getting signed, to the UFC. At the very least, it would get you top billing at a regional promotion. And, frankly, after winning ADCC there was nowhere left to go in the world of No-Gi grappling. While an ADCC medal was prestigious, no one made enough money to retire after winning one. Especially back then, there were very few grappling promotions where you could make any decent money. The "sub only" movement hadn't even begun yet, and no one was getting signed to long-term contracts. In fact, grapplers were often expected to pay to compete.

In those days, each professional jiu-jitsu organization could send a single competitor to the trials. And at Team Renzo Gracie, it was determined that the best way to choose our trials combatant was to fight it out amongst ourselves.

Yes, you read that right. A tournament to determine who could compete in the tournament that determined who competes in *the* tournament. I was a known commodity in the Renzo team; everyone knew I could very well win the in-house tournament. But I don't think anyone was betting money on me either. There were some big names in Team Renzo Gracie by 2007. His academy in the city was now an organization spanning the world. Matt Serra (fresh off the upset of the decade against Georges St-Pierre), Roger Gracie (who had just won the Absolute Division of the IBJJF World Championships), Ricardo Almeida, Braulio Estima, and more than a few others.

Renzo put the call out: if you wanted to represent Team Renzo Gracie, there would be a secret tournament in New York. No students, no media, no social media announcements. Show up in No-Gi attire, learn the ADCC rules, and plan to be at the Academy all day.

So on a Saturday afternoon, after the morning classes were done and everyone had eaten their lunch, eight of us showed up in midtown Manhattan. Renzo sat us all down and reviewed the rules. It was an eight-man tournament; three wins got you the spot. Renzo would referee each match. He reminded us that we were brothers, and brothers can fight each other but they never tell Mom and Dad what happened. It was his way of swearing us to secrecy. No one would be caught dead bragging about what happened this afternoon. Even to this day, I've never told anyone.

So I can't tell you who I fought that Saturday afternoon. But I can tell you how I felt. As we all took a knee on the mat, listening to Renzo talk, we stole little glances at each other. Some of us knew each other well. Many others were "out-of-towners" we knew from reputation but had never fought. We all sized each other up. Everyone in the room was a champion; some of them were world champions. Even those guys sized up the firepower in the room. People had travelled a long way to be here. As Renzo drew the brackets on a white board, everyone made eye contact with their first opponent.

No one seemed worried about me whatsoever.

It annoyed me that no one was giving me a hard swallow seeing my name be written down. I had fought for years to get respect. But as the lone purple belt, with no world titles and a 1–1 amateur MMA record, it was easy to confuse what I had done with what I was capable of.

As we all settled into various corners of the room to warm up, I felt a sort of calm rage. Being angry doesn't help in jiu-jitsu. This was different, more focused. I didn't hate any of these guys. I didn't even blame them for sleeping on me. But I knew that, even if I didn't win this thing, I *could* win it. I belonged here, and I knew in my heart that I was going to surprise some people today.

This feeling of focus settled in deeper as I watched guys taping their hands, hopping up and down, popping their necks. It was the power that you get from being an underdog, the indignant rage from knowing that you are being underestimated. But I wasn't going to be a warm-up round. I had been training with Renzo and his team for years by now. My time in the barrel was done.

I won't tell you that I went out there and smoked everyone. What happened in those next two or three hours was a war of attrition. After my first win, everyone was genuinely happy for me. *Let the kid win one* was the look their faces said. My second win was a prolonged one, where I couldn't help but glance at the onlookers from time to time. Their postures went from leaning back to leaning forward intensely. Some of them fidgeted with their hands, others covered their mouths while they uttered to the person next to them. They had gotten serious, because they knew I was serious.

At the end of the second match, I had my hand raised from Renzo. The half of the room that was already out of the tournament cheered loudly. The four competitors that were still in it applauded, but I could see their minds recalculating for this unexpected turn of events. All of them were recalibrating their mental scenario to include fighting me, not the favorite I had just beaten.

The last match was in a dead quiet room. There were no coaches or fans, only fighters who had taken their shot and lost. Even Renzo, normally immune to the pressure of the moment, burrowed his eyes into us during the match.

We were tired and fought a methodical tactical match. At this level, no one really gets exhausted. You recover fast but often have a little less in the tank as the day goes on. That last match was pure jiu-jitsu, none of the explosions of power and frantic scrambles that had characterized the previous fights. He caught a lead early, but I worked my way back into the fight. The match turned a corner, and I took a late lead. It was enough. My hand got raised.

Renzo told everyone, "This is the one we're sending to ADCC. This is Team Renzo right here." The other competitors could finally show their excitement. There was no bad blood or controversy. Everyone shook my hand; most people hugged me. I had always been confident, but having validation of your skills in such an undisputable fashion does wonders for your mental strength. On that day, I was the top grappler at the Renzo Gracie Academy. Maybe tomorrow there would be a different outcome, but I didn't have to be the top dog tomorrow. Just today.

I spent the next few weeks preparing for the ADCC North American Trials. There were hundreds of competitors registered, probably about two dozen in my weight class. The ADCC ruleset allows for very long matches, and I would go through several of them in order to win. ADCC rules also favored wrestling; pulling guard was penalized. So I developed that skill set as much as possible.

I prepared myself for the mental, physical, and even spiritual ordeal of fighting the best grapplers on the continent probably over the course of several hours. I trained as hard as I ever have. I wish I could say that I wanted to win more than anything in the world, but it's not entirely true. I had won the Renzo tournament; I deserved to be there. But a part of me still felt like now, I needed to win the trials. I had beaten some former, current, and future champions to get here. Losing the trials would be an insult to them—particularly losing to people that I knew they could have beaten.

It was the most pressure I had felt in my life. All of the strengths that got me here were now weaknesses. To win the Renzo tournament, I had drawn strength from being underestimated. But now, I worried people put too much faith in me.

This fear was a hell of a motivator during training. It became absolutely unacceptable to be anything but the hardest-working person in the tri-state area, especially in the Renzo team. If a teammate could stay late, I could stay later. If someone could do a hundred push-ups, I could do a hundred and one. It was the burden of being the flagbearer. I felt like an ancient barbarian warlord: as long as I could best everyone in combat at all times, I could continue leading the clan. But there are consequences to that.

A week before the trials, I noticed an occasional pop in my knee. Perpetually injured, I shoved negative thoughts aside. Everything popped, everything was sore. If you thought about every bump and bruise in training, you would be thinking a lot. I also knew that sometimes it's better not to know about the nature of certain injuries. It's easy to shrug off a "banged-up" knee, harder when you know the extent of the damage.

But as the days went on, I was forced to admit that I had a real problem. I couldn't extend my knee sometimes, and other times it would seem to lock in place. Pain, I could handle. But having knees that didn't work on command was a problem. Fortunately, there wasn't a ton of pain. But I had to know what I was dealing with. I saw a doctor, and an hour later I was staring at my MRI results while a doctor explained to me what a meniscus tear was.

I told the doctor that I was competing in a matter of days. I tried, and failed, to explain to this New Jersey doctor what the Abu Dhabi Combat Championship was and why I was going to still do it.

"I'm sorry," he said. "It's just not going to be safe to put any strain on it."

I stared at him, perplexed and annoyed at his pitiful definition of safety. He probably thought cars without at least four airbags weren't safe.

But all I said was, "I'm doing it. We can start rehab in two weeks."

The doctor gave me the same confused look I had just given him. I didn't argue with him. We were from two different worlds. This was a guy who had probably been working in the same office for twenty years in Jersey. His whole life was safe. I could never explain to him why jiu-jitsu was important to me, that it was saving me from depression and maybe even suicide at times. I didn't need to convince him. I'd come back to rehab with a medal around my neck.

CHAPTER 11

I would have liked to tell no one about my torn meniscus. But what made the injury serious was that it legitimately affected my performance. I kept training, but I could see Ricardo, who had known me for years at this point, eyeing me closely. He could see that I wasn't training as hard in the final week before training, and he knew something was up; I wasn't lazy. I didn't need to go into all the dirty details with him. Everyone had suffered injuries, and suffered through them.

The hardest part about being hurt is that it's a ready-made justification for losing. Many competitors have been known to hedge their bets prior to a match by making it known they are not quite one hundred percent. We hated these people, who often discredit their opponents with the implication that they were not fighting someone at their best. Our solution was that we rarely discussed injuries. The only injury was the one that stopped you from standing, walking, or fighting. Anything else was a bullshit excuse. Everyone fought hurt. Welcome to combat sports.

I'm not saying it was the healthiest mindset, just that it was the mentality at the time. Quitting wasn't an option for me. I was representing a whole team of people. I deserved to be there. I eventually told Ricardo about my injury. He reacted stoically, never once suggesting that I not compete. He made some suggestions about tactics and never showed doubt. But we both knew the reality: Wrestling was a key part of victory in ADCC. You needed functioning knees to wrestle. I had a strong bottom game, though; my half guard was well known at Renzo's. I had more than a shot.

The morning of the tournament, I was resolved. I had gotten better and better at dealing with nerves over time. Nothing can compare to the anxiety of an MMA fight, where a serious injury is realistically on the table. My own injury loomed in my mind, particularly as I eyed a hundred competitors checking in, showing IDs, signing waivers. They looked healthy; they looked fresh. In reality, they were probably as banged up as I was. But my mind was on the defensive.

It was my first MMA fight all over again. I knew and didn't know at the same time that my chances of performing well were not good. They say that an army must have unity to move with one purpose. That day, my mind didn't have that unity. I alternated between hope and despair, realism and fantasy.

My first match was against a black belt, which didn't intimidate me. I was one of the few non–black belts competing at trials. As I warmed up, the great Renzo Gracie walked up to me. The man couldn't walk more than twenty feet without someone stopping him to shake his hand or take a picture. Renzo lived his life in the moment, and he had to, with so many people fighting for his attention. I knew why: when Renzo talked to you, you felt good. He was a living belly laugh, the Brazilian Buddha. He told me that Ricardo had not been able to make it, which crushed me. Then he told me something that might have made me feel special in another time, but it just crushed me again: Renzo would corner me instead.

I walked on the mat just about as stressed as I had ever been in my life. I knew I was going to win; I had to. But just how the hell was I going to do it? I didn't know, but I shoved any thought of losing way down in my gut. I didn't think about the fallout or how it might not be that bad. Losing might as well have been death: a black nothingness that you weren't even aware was happening.

I took the center of the mat aggressively while my opponent walked comfortably, easing into his low stance. He wiped his hands on his shorts for no particular reason, but something about it bothered me. Everything about him bothered me. He gave a hundred little signs that he was a veteran. He either didn't know who I was or didn't respect me anyways. I was itchy, on a hair trigger. I circled him like a lion circles prey. As I closed the distance, his crouch got lower to the ground, as if he almost considered pulling guard but stopped just short. He was too low to change levels on, but also too low to keep his balance. I surged in and tackled him to the ground. I was greeted by a messy tangle of arms and legs, some of them mine and some his. He moved his four limbs with common purpose and coordination. I immediately realized he was a guard player, no doubt inviting me to take him down. His hips stayed elevated, and he began rolling on his back with practiced dexterity. He hands probed my defenses, feeling limbs and gauging reaction times while being careful to stay under me where I would have trouble settling.

I attacked as well, but in a more singular way. I concentrated my mind on lowering my base, applying pressure, and pinning him flat to pass his legs. I would isolate his hips, take away his movement, and then slowly gain ground. You had a generous amount of time in ADCC rules. Eventually, I would grind him out.

But as I set myself to this task, his seemingly purposeless gyrations suddenly felt more intentional as he secured a grip on my wrist, then quickly wrapped his arm around mine to lock it in. It was a fast and tight kimura. My arm was already extended from my guard pass attempt. The early answer to a kimura is to bring your elbows in tight. It was too late for that. It was time to move. If you're fast and smooth, you can "outrun" a kimura before your opponent can secure control over your lower body. I rolled over his body and tried to ewrench my arm free in the transition. He held on tight and flowed into the position with me. I was in a worse position now, still in a kimura grip but now from the bottom. I twisted my body a second time to my side, hoping to at least salvage the position so he would not be in mount.

I vaguely heard Renzo barking commands rapidly. In this particular sequence, a coach can only do so much. The path out of the kimura is one of movement and timing. It happened fast.

To my surprise, he let me back up and on top of him, only this time, his legs locked around my lower back. He had correctly valued his true prize as being the kimura lock, not the top position. I had taken back the top only to fall into an even worse predicament. If I stayed here, he would attack my shoulder until its various connective tissues tore. The pain would be terrible, and lasting. My movement options were limited. I could roll again to my back, giving him the mount position for sure this time, and he would still have the kimura lock.

While I considered this, the choice was abruptly taken out of my hands. A sharp pain began to increase exponentially as my shoulder exceeded its limits of motion. I instinctually tapped.

Cheers erupted from the stands. It was the first submission of the day, and the first time I had ever been submitted in competition. And it all happened in front of Renzo Gracie.

It was the worst moment of my career—even worse than my first MMA fight, which was terrible. I had bumped off eight elite fighters to be here. I was supposed to be the best man Renzo could put forth to represent him. People may not have expect me to win; no one can really expect you to win in a tournament this competitive. But I was expected to progress and at least win my first match.

Renzo clapped me on the back and cheerfully told me that I had done my best or something like that. I'm sure he was sincere, but his attitude made me feel a hundred times worse. He talked to me like one might talk to a child that had lost his first kids' tournament, like he was just happy I showed up. I would have almost preferred the seriousness of Ricardo, who would have been disappointed *because* he had such high expectations of me. Renzo's reaction made me wonder if he had expected this all along. Had he known about the injury and adjusted his expectations accordingly?

In truth, the injury had little impact on the fight. Sure, I may have trained much more in the final weeks, but the fight itself had played out on equal footing. My opponent simply had my number.

The next week, I returned to the doctor. I was hoping he would have completely forgotten our little exchange. But how could he forget it? He immediately asked how my tournament went. I told him that it went fine, and he took the hint without asking further questions. But I did catch a brief look of appraisal in his eyes.

That Monday, walking back into the evening class at Renzo's was one of the harder walks I've had to make. The fighters were all professional and stoic; many of them said nothing and probably had thought little about it. But I read into everyone's comments of sympathy and encouragement. I couldn't help but look at everyone in the room and feel as if nearly everyone could have gotten further into the ADCC Trials than I did. I felt sorry for myself for a few days and then refocused my self-pity into a righteous anger. If people thought I was going back to the kiddie pool, they were in for a rude awakening. The next ADCC trials was in two years. I would take my revenge.

CHAPTER 12

My phone rings, and I glance at the name on the screen, it's one I haven't heard from in awhile. A guy from the neighborhood. I pick it up and we exchange small talk for a minute before the voice tells me that he just saw something I should know about. I listen incredulously before saying, "Naw, my Dad?"

"Yeah man, I'm pretty sure it was him."

"Walking down the side of the highway?"

"Yeah, going towards the Rite Aid."

I thought of the image of my father, hobbling down a busy road. With all his ailments, it seemed impossible. I say to the voice on the other end, "I mean, this dude can barely walk to the mailbox nowadays. You said he was—when was this?"

"It was five minutes ago, dude. Maybe less."

I glance at the clock in my truck. My private lesson starts in ten minutes. I mentally shift through the staff at the academy in this hour. One of my top students, a black belt, is there now finishing up a class. I make a snap decision. I won't be at this private lesson. I will call my instructor and ask him to fill in. I hate missing a commitment, and I'll make it up to my student. But if my father's in some sort of trouble, obviously the play is to turn this truck around. I can be back in the neighborhood in twenty minutes.

"Okay, hey, I'm gonna swing back into town to find him. Thanks a lot, I really appreciate you calling me."

I hang up and take the next exit. The image of my father as a helpless old man wandering around in Jersey causes my foot to hit the gas a little harder. For no particular reason, I reach out and touch the old metal dog tags hanging from my rearview window. I had just driven him to the clinic this morning; he hadn't mentioned anything about needing to go out and run errands. We just talked about the story. What was it? Ah, yes: my second MMA fight. The one where I got things right this time.

I'm coming, Dad.

———•———

Fighters talk about "embracing the grind," and it's absolutely true. Kurt Pellegrino would sometimes talk about not living like a real fighter before you actually became one. I was taking that to heart (for the time being). My life was a training montage. Four days a week, I would wake up at 4:30 and drive an hour to Ricardo's house. From there, we'd drive an hour and a half to a gym for a two-hour training session. After that, we'd drive an hour and a half to Renzo's Academy in New York. Another two-hour training session. Drive back to Ricardo's house. I'd take a nap, train for another hour, and then drive back home.

I would do this four days a week. The other three, I needed to make money. I took up becoming a schoolteacher. I had finished college with my degree in education. I took a job at a special education school right out of college, teaching severely autistic children. I had always wanted to be a special education teacher because of my own issues learning when I was a child. I had been diagnosed with ADD when I was very young. In the '80s, ADD was barely recognized as a learning disability. Instead, you were more likely to be told plainly by students, or teachers, that you were just stupid (this was Jersey, after all). It would take me hours to do simple homework assignments. When I started high school I was evaluated to be at a third-grade level across the board: math, reading, writing, everything. Three years into high school, I had caught up and even discovered that I enjoyed reading and writing. But it was hard to shake the feeling that maybe I really *was* stupid. After all, I was good at sports, and I liked to fight people. There was a stereotype that people like that couldn't *also* be smart.

You may think that I couldn't possibly have been good with kids. An amateur fighter prone to depression? But I actually was. I loved kids. I had "the switch"—the ability to be funny and patient and turn off the part of me that could fight to the death. I worked with autistic kids for one year, then became a public school teacher for three years, training every moment I wasn't at school. I taught a class of fourth-graders, which I genuinely loved. Fourth graders are, mostly, a fun age group: old enough to have fun with and teach a thing or two about life, but young enough that they are still bright-eyed kids.

One of my kids was so autistic that she didn't move on her own accord. She would remain in a place until I took her hand and guided her to another part of the room. Once there, she would stay there no matter what.

Another kid, his name was Quasi. He was fifteen but already taller and bigger than me. He was a mountain, and he had the intelligence of a three-year-old. On days where he was happy to see me, he would run at me and put an arm around my shoulder, pulling me close and making loud noises. Despite all my training, he had such raw strength he inadvertently manhandled me most of the time.

It was a contrast, spending the days playing games and herding kids in from recess, then going to a very different playground where grown men try to kill each other.

It was the same duality I had experienced all my life. My dad would be drinking all night; then I would go to school the next day with a smile on my face. There was a price to pay for all of this, though. I'd love to tell you that I was "on purpose" doing what I love. And it's true, I felt like fighting was my calling even if I didn't yet see the pathway to fame and fortune (no one was getting rich off fighting back then). But at the same time, I knew I was unwell. My depression that I had battled with for most of my life had never really gone away. In fact, maybe it had gotten worse. My loneliness had also grown. I probably don't have to tell you that the guys I was seeing day in and day out were not the most emotionally open people. They weren't bad guys; in fact, some of them might have been supportive and helpful had I spoken to them. But in their world, fighting and training were the solutions to everything. The constant war we waged at the gym was a way to deal with our various issues. And, to be honest, it wasn't always particularly effective. I learned that training could be a healthy activity, but it wasn't a cure for the deeper issues that men have. In the Renzo Gracie team, as I got to know my training partners better, I realized that many of the guys there were unwell in ways that they hid just as well as me.

In desperation, I went to my mother. I told her I needed help, that something was wrong with me. She was one hundred percent supportive, and on a Friday morning I checked myself into one of those places that they never call a mental hospital, but that's what it is.

I can tell you that after three days at that place, I'm not a huge fan of the New Jersey institutional system. But maybe it's no worse than any other. I quickly came to understand there are levels to mental illness, several of them higher than whatever I was dealing with. I saw people that were battling severe personality disorders, crippling narcissism, and mental disabilities. These were people that would never have normal lives, maybe never leave the facility. They were simply put there, where they couldn't be seen or remembered. I felt like the purpose of the hospital was as much to hide them from society as anything.

As I observed the people around me, doctors and specialists interviewed me. With each question they asked, I felt embarrassed. I didn't belong here. I wasn't a danger to others. I wasn't mentally paralysed; I wasn't socially unable to function. I was depressed, that's all. I left the facility after the weekend. Monday morning, I came back to class. I acted like nothing happened.

It's a terrible thing, to measure your sickness against someone else's. For years after, I believed that my depression didn't deserve help, because it wasn't as serious as other people's. It reinforced my feeling that hiding was the solution. So that became my game plan. Hide the real Tom. Even if that meant hiding the real Tom . . . from the real Tom.

In my team, virtually everyone was always training for the fight of their life. We took it seriously, but at the same time I felt no pressure from the team, just myself. I didn't have to uphold the Gracie name or have tens of thousands of dollars on the line. But I *was* expected to win. Everyone was.

Early in my competition career, I competed in the expert division as a purple belt. I fought brown and black belts and came in second place after three wins. I was happy with myself. I had punched above my weight; I was only a purple belt, but I had *belonged* in that division. I'll never forget walking up to Ricardo after the match with a shit-eating grin on my face.

"You lost," he said matter-of-factly.

To Ricardo, winning wasn't relative. You won or you lost. He grew up fighting, first in the streets of Brazil, then in the cage or ring. Second place was just another loser to him. From that moment on, it became the same for me. I came home with a gold medal, or I didn't. If it sounds harsh, it's not, if you want to be a champion. Some people are happy with silver or bronze, and that's fine. Even today, certain students of mine make it to the podium and I praise them. They went out there and competed, win or lose. But other students, the ones that tell me they want to be champions, don't get that treatment. I treat them the way Ricardo treated me. You have to hate losing. The very thought of it gets you up early to hit the gym or keeps you up an extra hour at night.

I became that person. I expected to win. I was a Ricardo Almeida student. I was part of the Renzo Gracie team. I was going to pull my weight. I took that obsessive part of my brain, the part that liked shitty things, and put it to work. In a way, it was what all of us did. We took that messed-up psychology we all had and unleashed it into something positive. It gave us all an edge, the fact that we were crazy. That we would train all night, then get home and go for a run.

After my humiliating ADCC loss, I had more reason than most to adopt this approach. ADCC was every two years, meaning that I could not compete in the trials for some time. Nothing could replace winning the ADCC trials, but maybe winning everything else would come close.

I was awarded my brown belt around this time. I had been fighting black belts for years, and I wanted to compete against black belts, the biggest names in the sport. I certainly didn't want to fight purple belts. Right around the time I hit brown belt, I went from winning most of the time to winning nearly all of the time. I was training with black belts every day, world-class ones. My body was reaching its athletic peak, and my skills were rapidly improving. I was starting to settle into my fighting style as well. Although I had started my career as an aggressive, top-game fighter, years of being mauled by Kurt, Ricardo, Renzo, and his brothers and cousins had prompted me to develop a guard game.

The closed guard is most commonly the first position that students learn in jiu-jitsu. It's not just effective, it has a whole historical significance. But it's not the only tool in the toolbox. I had notoriously short legs. It was difficult to wrap them around many of my sparring partners. A closed guard that doesn't close isn't very useful, but closing my legs around someone's leg was always possible. My legs were short but strong, and I could always hold an opponent at bay from this new position. Of course, it was the half guard.

At this time in jiu-jitsu, the idea of the offensive, active half guard was in its infancy. Most fighters saw half guard as a mere transitional position. In my team, there was one fighter, a black belt named Steven Kim, who had turned the half guard into an art form. Steven was a full-time part-timer, meaning that he had a career as a law student (and later attorney) outside of training yet still trained almost every night. He was an accomplished tournament fighter, having won the 2003 Mundials, among others. He was a quiet, polite and unassuming man but a serial killer on the mats.

He was a thinking man's fighter: slow, methodical, and technical. If Ricardo was the "big dog," Kim was the "big snake," slowly wrapping himself around and around while tightening his grip. I had seen many fighters wade into his half guard only to become confused by his unconventional half guard sweeps and subsequent attacks. I used the phrase *serial killer* because he enjoyed dismantling people, and he did it coolly.

He was probably a great lawyer.

I rolled with Kim a lot, picking up pointers about his half guard game. I learned that half guard is a crossroads to many other positions. A fighter with a dangerous half guard was dangerous from everywhere. Over time, Kim began picking up on the fact that I was trying to mimic his game. He would occasionally drop hints after a roll, telling me that I had come close—if only I had grabbed the toes instead of the ankle, for example. I never really could get Kim's number, but my success around the gym continued to improve.

My first year at brown belt, I won the Nationals. Then I won the Pan American Championship. I decided to try my luck at No-Gi jiu-jitsu, and I won the No-Gi Worlds. I'll never say it was easy. All of them were hard; all of them took chunks of my life energy in training. But I will say that mentally, they all became easier. The first time ever that you taste meat, it makes you sick. But after a while you get a taste for it. I had become a meat-eater. My name was starting to be floated around as *a guy* in the Renzo Gracie team, not just another training partner for the guys. Now, when people talked about who was at the Renzo Gracie team, I had a name. They would say, "You know, the Renzo Gracie team with Matt Serra and Georges St-Pierre, Ricardo Almeida and Tom DeBlass."

It's true, my name didn't carry the weight of some of the others on that list yet. But people in the know knew about me by now. Maybe I was just a jiu-jitsu guy for now. But that would start to change soon.

I was starting to experience real success. But privately, I floated in and out of despair. Every win was a relief from my depression, but every win was temporary. My life was an unsustainable formula. Fight and win to distract myself, to take the edge off. When I couldn't compete, the edge still needed to go away somehow. In those times, my outlets became less healthy. I would go to parties, go to strip clubs, stay up all night. Anything to keep me busy. If you would have forced me to sit on a couch with nothing but my own thoughts, I might have gone insane. Many people say they find themselves through martial arts. I was avoiding myself, my own private thoughts, my past. I needed every tournament to be the biggest one possible, the one that would require one hundred percent of my focus and mental attention. Then, I wouldn't need to spend time with myself. But I also recognized that the cycle would end eventually. I couldn't compete forever, couldn't train forever. My pain would *never* stop coming for me. It would catch up with me. I sometimes wondered if death was the solution.

CHAPTER 13

It doesn't take long to find him, an old man shambling back from the Rite Aid. I catch up with him just a few blocks from home. There's a small paper bag in his hand. The mild panic I felt during the drive dissipates and gives way to confusion first, and then anger. I played Russian roulette with a lot of traffic laws to get here, driven on by images of my Dad lost or in danger.

But he's fine. More than fine, actually. He's high as a kite. He didn't even wait to get home to open the box of Benadryl. Popped two on his way home. He rambles a bit, coming up with some pretense for being out. Picking apart the holes in his story seems like a waste of time when he's high. In fact, it's almost a waste of time when he's sober. God looks after fools and old men, and my father has cheated death too many times to stop now. When I was younger, I used to yell at him, get angry. But it gets hard to yell at a shriveled old man, nodding in and out of it on the car ride home.

In my academy, when a student fucks up I can tell them. I can tell them what they did wrong, what the consequences will be, and what they need to do to make it right. But now, as I get Dad settled on the couch and see him sweating from the heat and dimly aware of me, none of those things can happen. I can't tell him what he did wrong because I've been telling him his whole life. I can't think of any consequence that he hasn't already lived through. And I can't tell him how to make it right because I'm not going to get my hopes up again.

I plead with him a little, scold him a little. I resolve to have a deeper talk with him later, when he's clear-eyed. I glance at my phone to see a flood of emails and messages. The world doesn't stop, and I think of my mother telling me that no matter what happens in your life, you have to work.

I sit there for a minute or two. He's nodded off again, and I say to no one in particular, "You know I almost killed myself—" I pause, not sure if I should say "for you" or "because of you." I think about it for a minute, but I have to get back. Mom will be home in thirty minutes, so I leave and get back to Ocean County Jiu Jitsu.

Ocean County is in many ways a major relationship in my life. It's a long-term relationship, with ups and downs and children of a sort. It's my home, my business, and my family all wrapped up in one. Unlike other businesses, you cannot close for the day. It's a business of relationships, hundreds of them. You have to show up, every day, no matter what. Even if your father has to get dropped of at home for awhile. It's not an easy life, but I knew what I was getting into when I started Ocean County.

———•———

Jiu-jitsu was changing. Every week, people would wander into classes at Ricardo's or Renzo's academies, wanting to take a class. We would watch these prospects like hardened prisoners evaluating new inmates. Years of rough training had made us all proud of our skills and mental toughness. Jiu-jitsu wasn't for everyone, and we were proud that we had survived. I and the others could tell instantly whether a new student would stay or not. We profiled every person that came in. And while we were occasionally surprised, we almost always called it right. Guys that looked tough, were strong, and had a little chip on their shoulder would often stay. Everyone else would normally leave. Jiu-jitsu was the law of the jungle: only the strong survive.

There was a certain Darwinistic beauty in this. We didn't have to come down to anyone's level; they had to come up to ours. If you could learn to keep up with the pack, you had something to contribute. In my case, my initial contribution was simple toughness. I was a good training partner that would go as long as my partners were willing. I didn't complain, I didn't give up. Eventually, my contributions expanded. I became skilled in certain areas, like my half guard. By the time I was a purple belt, students were coming to me to learn skills, even students with more experience overall.

But the "law of the jungle" mentality didn't think about what *we* were contributing to each other. Every new sign-up was human firewood to the top guys. I *liked* this system. I wanted to fight. I didn't like holding back so that others' feelings could be spared. That's why I had left Taekwondo.

But I couldn't help but feel a pang of guilt as I saw students leave after a week or two of ass-kickings. I saw people come into the academies that were smart, talented, educated, or just good people. We were losing something when we ran them out. We had academies with great fighters, but could we help kids that were being bullied or adults that needed some more confidence?

Not only that, but I also had the sneaking suspicion that many of our discarded prospects actually had a lot of potential. Maybe there *were* some wolves among the sheep, they just needed a little more time to come into their own. Every now and again, a student would confirm these suspicions. I remember a pasty-looking kid that started training at Renzo's. He was nothing special; you barely noticed him other than to occasionally glance over and wonder why he was still around. He didn't talk much, opting to listen so intensely it weirded the rest of us out. In fact, for the first few years I knew him, I only ever heard his voice when he was asking questions, which he did after virtually every technique demonstration in his strange accent. The guy wasn't particularly large or strong, but he proved to be impossible to get rid of. While guys like me got off on the raw kineticism of jiu-jitsu, this guy was sort of a nerd. Jiu-jitsu was a science to him. Before long, he was surprisingly good. He developed a reputation as the guy that could explain anything.

He was an example of how an academy is made better by taking in different types of people and giving them a long enough runway to take off. I watched these students and thought about myself as a teenager. I had needed help, and maybe jiu-jitsu could have been an answer, but my mother would never sign me up for a school where I would be fighting grown adults.

These were the first seeds planted in my head that maybe I could start my own academy. It would be different than the kill-or-be-killed environment I had started out in. I was spending my days as a schoolteacher, helping kids learn confidence. I had to push them outside their comfort zones, but never too far too fast. I thought every day about how teaching kids wasn't all that different from teaching jiu-jitsu to adults. Your first day on the mats is like your first day at a new school. You hope the other kids are nice and that you won't look like an idiot. Just like a good teacher would help you get started, a good jiu-jitsu instructor would make sure you were training the right techniques with the right people. I knew I could be that instructor. When I saw people leave and never come back, I thought about how I might have tried to keep them in the gym instead of saying "good riddance."

I had started teaching at Ricardo's as a purple belt. I taught the smaller, beginner classes. I thought it would be a grind, teaching simple escapes and armbars day after day. But I actually loved it. Advanced students don't need teachers in the same way. They need trainers, people to give their sessions focus and direction. But a brand-new student can still see the magic of jiu-jitsu. Teaching them is like being the parent of a newborn. Every day, there are huge milestones to celebrate. I got great satisfaction from seeing these students break through to a new level, and I wanted more.

Most teachers would laugh at a twenty-four-year old purple belt asking about starting his own academy. Ricardo was forward-thinking, though. He didn't see my rank—he saw my potential, and I've always been grateful for that. At the time, my belt was more of a formality. I was training with pro fighters, most of them black belts and world champions, and I was doing it every day. I wasn't a belt chaser. The belts were chasing me, if anything.

I was young, but most people were surprised to hear just how young I was. I had become a serious man. It's not that I never laughed or never enjoyed myself. But I didn't do the stupid things that would have given my age away. I trained and I worked.

Ricardo invited me to come to the instructor meetings, which were normally about an hour long. It added yet another hour on the mats to my day. I would teach my grade-schoolers most of the day, drive an hour and a half to Ricardo's gym, take an hour and a half class, teach my own class for an hour, train MMA for an hour, and finally sit in the instructor's class for an hour. We often left the school around eleven at night.

While Ricardo was supportive when I told him I wanted to open an academy, he probably didn't expect me to find an office space the very next week. But that's exactly what I did. I signed a lease with virtually no savings and no way to pay the rent. I rung up $20,000 on a credit card, which covered mats, a deposit on the space, and some other essentials. I was like the old explorers, burning their own ships upon landfall. Rapid success was the plan. In six months, I'd either have more students that I had space for or I'd be out of business. It was my style. I liked pressure; I liked high stakes.

Not that I'm recommending you do this. Being $20,000 in credit-card debt probably wasn't the smartest thing, in hindsight. But starting an academy on that budget was actually fairly lean. Some people rent huge spaces or make renovations. I took a more conservative route: start small and keep going until you outgrow your space, then get a bigger one and repeat the process.

My space, which I had decided to call Ocean County BJJ (keep it simple, right?) was better suited to be a dentist's office or a barber shop. It was tiny, just a few hundred square feet. Hell, it wasn't even the right shape. It was kind of a L shape, meaning that I would have to teach in one room and then split a class. I would need to go from one room to another; I could never see more than half my students at one time. There was no hot water, no changing room, and sure as hell no storage. The capstone to my little project was a large cardboard sign I put above the building that read "Ocean County BJJ."

It was perfect, the most beautiful thing I had ever owned (okay, I didn't even own it). Where others saw a shithole, I saw freedom. I saw a place with no boss, no uniform, no warnings for tardiness, and, best of all, no limits. I was a good teacher from a reputable school and the only dedicated BJJ school within twenty miles. If I succeeded, I would get one hundred percent of the credit (and profit). If I failed, I would be one hundred percent responsible.

So instead of spending a few hours at my middle school, then a few hours at Ricardo's, a few at Renzo's, and several just driving from place to place, I now spent most of that time in my academy. I still taught my grade-schoolers, but everything else became very curtailed. It was a one-room palace, but I pretended it was the world headquarters of an empire of jiu-jitsu schools. I would teach a class of one student like there was a hundred. I cleaned the mats every day, I started every class on time. If the very first student showed up at ten after, I would say, "You're late, we already started," even if the "we" was just myself. It was fake-it-til-you-make-it. But leadership starts at the top. I carried myself a certain way, and that first wave of students followed suit. Just because we were in a shitty building didn't mean we were a shitty school. We weren't a school at all. We were an *academy*. That meant a clean mat space, where people wore fresh uniforms, followed the rules I made, and committed to getting better, whatever "better" meant for them.

In two months, I had enough money to rent a storefront location. In four months, I had 150 students and quit my job.

CHAPTER 14

"I know what you're thinking, son." My Dad's voice had a cautionary tone.

I mumbled something reassuring to keep him at bay, but I was staring hard out the window, going into a different place in my mind.

We were parked at a gas station in Jersey, taking my Dad to the methadone clinic like always, but today my daughter was with us so I could drop her off at a friend's house. After filling up, I watched another car pull up—tinted windows, blaring music, pulled into the gas station at like thirty miles an hour. The car had to stop short behind another car and wait for a pump to open up.

Young punk gets out. Maybe I was already peeved about him driving up that fast with my daughter in the car, but the guy just *walks* like an asshole. One of those guys who walks like there is music in his head that only he can hear. In Jersey, we have full-service gas stations, so someone works at the gas station and fills up your car while you wait. An elderly man, and I mean elderly, hobbles up to the car, painfully slow, and begins to unwind the gas cap. I don't think much of it. Jersey is filled with assholes as well as saints. I walk into the station to grab a water.

A few minutes pass. I lose myself briefly in the heated comfort of the gas station. Cheerful music plays, and two attendants bust each other's balls about the game last night. I pay inside and walk back out. Outside, it's New Jersey again, and Punk has had enough of waiting:

"Put the fucking cap on the right way so we can get out of here!"

The old man nods quickly and says, "Yes sir, okay, yes sir," over and over. He puts his hand out to steady himself on the side of the car.

"You're gonna get grease all over my shit, dude!" The punk is walking around the driver's side to where the attendant is finishing up pumping. He has a walk that I don't like, for different reasons than the *last* walk I didn't like.

He walks like a crazy person. Or at least a violent one. He walks like he's going to get too close to someone or maybe shove them. The old man senses this, too, and recoils as he is approached. The gas cap slips out of his shaky hands, making a loud clatter on the ground, and does the worst possible thing for the situation: it rolls under the car.

"Jesus Christ, look what you did!" Punk is spreading his arms wide.

What he says next is a little muffled by the sound of my car door closing. I hand out the spoils: a lottery ticket for my Dad, an Abba-Zaba bar for my daughter, and water for me.

My father barely notices the commotion outside. He lives in Baylor, for God's sake. Someone could get stabbed outside and he wouldn't stop scratching his lottery ticket.

My daughter, though, is transfixed. Children are far less able to ignore suffering. They don't think about life choices or none-of-my-business stuff. She only can see an old man being mistreated. I look at her eyes and I see a genuine concern.

"Daddy, is that man being hurt?" she says matter-of-factly, like maybe I didn't notice because I'm obviously not out there doing something.

My father still hasn't looked up, "They're just arguing, sweetie," he says to her.

I turn my attention back outside and stare for a few seconds. We should be pulling out of the station, but we're not. That familiar feeling of righteous rage starts to well up. I look at the poor old man and see my dad, then my daughter, then myself as a five-year-old, getting pelted by rocks in the sand pit.

"I know what you're thinking, son," comes my Dad's voice.

"Hang on a second," I say as I open the car door.

I wish I could tell you that I stared the guy down as a tumbleweed blew across the gas station. That I said something in a low and menacing voice, Clint Eastwood–style, sending them fleeing in humiliation.

In reality, I'm pretty sure I said something like: "Hey, you gonna talk to this poor guy this way? Talk to me that way, you fucking pig!"

It wasn't poetry, but it got their attention. I say "their" because, in a few seconds, two other variations of Punk got out of the car, now making three people. None of them looked particularly dangerous, but they also looked perfectly willing to fight. But three on one is never good, even if the three are harmless individually.

I fell back on an old Renzo Gracie truism—not really purposefully, just because it's my nature: a crazy person is a scary person. Sane people can do math, size up their odds of surviving a three-on-one. Crazy people cannot. The three men were jeering at me now, and my anger was boiling over. I turned it up to eleven. "I will kill all three of you motherfuckers." I pointed at the first guy and looked him in the eye. "I will take your life, I swear to God."

He didn't back down, but I also saw his eyes scan me for the first time. His eyes lingered my shirt and what was written on it.

Ricardo Almeida MMA

There was a flicker of understanding in his eyes. More curses were exchanged. I'm not proud of the way I went about it, but I'm proud that I did something. I think it was when I told them that I would bite their faces off if I had to that they finally backed down. There was no apology or handshake, but they left, and that's what mattered.

I got back into the car. My Dad threw his hands up. "Jesus Christ, we're gonna be late now."

I looked back at my daughter. She was smiling, an Abba-Zabba hanging from her mouth.

"You scared them off, Daddy."

"I wasn't going to let them talk to him like that," I said. I wonder if she heard or understood all the words I used. Hopefully not, but her smile told me that it didn't matter. I had driven off the monsters. It's funny—I will do just about anything to live up to my daughter's expectations, but nothing to live up to my father's.

My phone rings. I check it and see it's Garry, one of my first students and my first black belt. I make a note to call him back.

My father observes and asks who was calling.

"It's Garry, one of my old students. I'll call him when I drop you off."

"Is he still fighting?" Dad asks.

"Oh yeah, the guy is huge now. MMA, jiu-jitsu, the guy is fucking incredible. I got some stories with him."

"Oh yeah? Tell me."

———— • ————

Over the years, a number of interesting characters would walk through the front doors of Ocean County BJJ. We welcomed everyone to the farm, where every animal survived. That meant skilled prospects and soccer moms. I would come to learn that it also included tweakers, gangsters, bums, crazy people, and people pretending to be all four. After all, this was New Jersey.

I didn't judge. As long as you followed my rules and your checks cleared, you were welcome at Ocean County BJJ (sometimes the checks didn't clear, and I welcomed you anyways). Crazy people didn't bother me. Quite the opposite: all the best fighters I knew were crazy. And I definitely was. My mats were a melting pot, as American as the Statue of Liberty. Doctors, kids, cops, and crooks, all working together.

One of the more colorful characters to walk through my doors was a teenager with long shaggy hair and a pockmarked face. He wandered into my gym and immediately annoyed me. He talked in a stream-of-consciousness fashion, changing subjects mid-sentence. He had no manners, barely any social skills, and some nasty ADHD.

I was a world-weary twenty-four-year-old. I had been through depression and addiction, and I'd seen incredible loss. I wasn't the most positive dude in the world. I was training all the time. I was serious.

Something about this kid annoyed me, and in an earnest effort to make him go away, I mauled him in our first training session. I figured if I didn't run him off for good, he would at least eat some humble pie and come back with a different attitude next time.

But to my disappointment, the kid was really tough. He didn't respond to losing the way he "should" have. He liked it. Not only did he come back the next day, but the shit-eating grin on his face remained. I beat him again, then threw a good blue belt on him. He was unfazed. He was a good wrestler from his high school days, and stupid enough that he didn't fear anyone and didn't respect being in bad positions.

His name was Garry Tonon.

Garry became the little brother I couldn't get rid of. He showed up for two classes a day for years. I decided that if I couldn't get rid of him, I would at least clean him up a little. Every time he showed up with a dirty gi or cranked a submission too hard, I was all over him. He didn't go away. Even worse, he started competing. He won some local NAGA tournaments as a white belt, using pure grit and resilience. He started bugging me about wanting to train on the weekends with Ricardo. I relented as long as I could until he followed me in the parking lot one night, talking my ear off about it.

"Fine," I told him. "I'll pick you up at seven."

Surprisingly, he was on time when I pulled up to his house before dawn. Garry jumped in the car, and I settled in for an awkward one-hour drive to Ricardo's. I couldn't decide what would be worse: a never-ending awkward silence, or Garry asking me a million questions about Ricardo. It was the latter. Garry wanted to know where it was, if Ricardo was cool, had I ever been to one of his UFC fights, would I ever fight in the UFC, would *he* ever fight in the UFC, and so on.

I got impatient and recalled seeing another car parked in his driveway. I asked why his parents couldn't take him next time. Garry shifted in his seat and mumbled that he would ask. He changed the subject.

I came from a loving home, but I also had an alcoholic father and a mother that would suffer crippling bouts of pain. I could tell when someone didn't want to talk about their parents.

In the months that followed, I got to know Garry better. He wasn't an idiot, his mind just worked a little differently. But I saw him slowly put everything together in jiu-jitsu, and I began to appreciate his creative side. The stupid things he tried seemed less and less stupid. In fact, I started wondering if he was some sort prodigy.

I also learned that Garry didn't have a particularly great home life, something I could relate to. His parents had divorced; he lived with his mother and his stepdad. He wasn't home a lot. Sometimes life gives you people whether you're ready or not. Garry probably should have come into my gym ten years later than he did. I was twenty-four when I met him. I was a serious competitor and hadn't yet settled into being a role model or a father figure. An older Tom would have become a father figure and a coach to the kid. Instead, I got more like an older brother, albeit a protective one that was loyal. As Garry endeared himself to me, I began to understand how good he could become, but even then he managed to surprise me for years to come. Little did I know, but that sixteen-year-old would become my first black belt and would be widely recognized as the best in the world for a time, only to be replaced by one of his own students, Gordon Ryan. But that's another story.

CHAPTER 15

"So he's talking to you, like, every night?"

I swallow a piece of ribeye and nod while clearing my throat. "Yeah, pretty much. We take little breaks, but we're talking all the time. We're writing it together."

"He sends him pictures of me!" Isabelle says, smiling with a spoonful of pasta in her mouth.

My father pauses and asks a clarifying question. "And it's about all your fights?"

"No, it's sort of gonna be about everything. It's like a biography."

"Ahh, your life story."

I nod, and the noise at the dinner table returns to the clinks of silverware and other sounds of an enjoyed meal: my mother scolding Thomas for grabbing food with his hands; Isabelle idly talking to no one in particular about her day. My father looks pensive as he stares at his plate. The news of the book deal is giving him some thoughts.

I catch him out of the corner of my eye and wait patiently for him to say what's on his mind. Which he eventually does, "You talk about us, about our family?"

I don't look up from my plate but feel his eyes burning into me, "Sure, yeah, we're talking about everything. I'm gonna be really open and honest. I've, uh, already told him a lot."

He raises an eyebrow. "What's 'a lot'?"

"Dad, a lot of people can be helped by this story. No one has been through everything that I have. I came from nothing, and now I'm one of the most successful people in this business—"

"Daddy, I want a soda!"

I pause to tell Thomas no and manage his brief flare of anger on being denied. While I do, my father slowly returns to eating, and I hope the conversation is tabled. Truthfully, I've held almost nothing back for the book. Even things I had planned to keep to myself, they just came out in the past few months, and we're not even done yet. If you talk to someone long enough and about enough things, everything comes out eventually. It took a long time before I brought up being molested or fighting with my Dad. I know that there's more to come—heavier stuff, even. But this guy writing it with me will find them all eventually. He has a way of getting it out of me. Some of the stories I'm ready for the world to hear. Others I may ask we leave out. I try and push myself. It's okay for people to see the messy truth. But sometimes, maybe it was too messy.

"Leave it, please!" My father had a pitiful look on his face as he pleaded with two nurses. They spoke to him in firm voices, using his name repeatedly.

"Tom. *Tom.* Listen to me. We need to put this in your arm. You need to calm down and let us help you."

Dad talks over them, hearing their voices but not their words. When he's not speaking, he gives a sort of moan not aimed at anyone or anything in particular. It's equal parts physical pain, chemical withdrawal, and all of the parts of his soul that fuel both.

"Please, don't take that. My son gave me that bracelet."

He says it over and over. *My son gave me that bracelet.* I've never given him a bracelet. He doesn't own a bracelet. He's wearing a hospital wristband, mass-produced and meaningless. But he has tears in his eyes as he waves his arms weakly to ward off the nurses. They are hardened healthcare workers. I am amazed how they can bury their empathy deep down when it's time to do a job. They may go cry in their cars during shift change, but right now they are focused and unaffected by his delusional rant.

Still, there must be some rule that they aren't allowed to wrestle a patient down. They avoid touching him. He already has cords and lines connected to him, connected to other machines. One of the nurses says to the other, "We may need to call security." As she says it, she throws the briefest of glances to me, and our eyes connect. In that one glance, I perceive that she's making an ask.

I don't know if it's appropriate or not, but I step forward. My strong, twenty-four-year-old hands grab his wrist, locking him tight like a vise. My father is the strongest man alive, as far as I know. Physically, I mean. But his brick-punching days are long behind him. Now, just hours after a heroin overdose, I easily pin his wrists down and begin speaking to him. It's not too different from the way I would speak to my special ed students, some of who would also act out and need to be physically restrained. It wasn't common, but it happened.

I look deep into my father's eyes and speak to him in slow, soothing tones. He gradually calms down, but he still doesn't fully get it.

"Please, my son got me this bracelet," he says to me.

"Dad, it's me. I'm here." I fight back tears.

The DeBlasses are resilient. My father has never overdosed. My mother is here; we embrace after Dad finally goes down. But there's not many tears. Nor is there any solemn vow that this will be the last time. Instead, there is just a feeling that we should get some rest to get ready for the next one. It could be a week, could be a year. Dad can always get clean, but no one expects him to stay clean.

I had shared my father with drugs and alcohol my entire life. I had been pleading with him to quit since I became aware of what addiction is. Now, in my twenties, I had acknowledged that he was an addict, and addicts never really stop. Acknowledging is not the same as accepting, however. There were times I accepted him, and other times I couldn't.

CHAPTER 16

I pick up my father the next day, in a sour mood. I thought a long time about the story of him overdosing last night after our conversation at the dinner table. How he had made a big deal out of that stupid bracelet. Part of me wants to use this drive to talk about it, but what is there to say, really? Does he even remember? I doubt it.

I don't get the chance. My father is invested now in what we are calling "the story." He always remembers where we left off and prompts me to continue soon after the car rides start every morning. He never lets on just how much he remembers or doesn't remember, and I don't feel like asking.

"So where are we today?" I grunt.

"Ahhh . . . okay, we talked about Garry and winning all that stuff at brown belt. So you went back to ADCC to kick ass, then?"

"Yes and no, I went back to the *trials*," I emphasize.

"What's the difference again?"

"The trials get you into ADCC, into the worldwide championship, but winning the trials is a big deal, just as hard as winning ADCC in a lot of ways."

"Plus, they were black belts. You were still a brown belt."

"Well, I *was* a black belt the second time around."

"Ah, really? Did we talk about you getting your black belt?"

"I guess not, but you were there, remember?"

"Of course I fucking remember!" he says loudly. He gets sensitive to the fact that he was absent, physically or mentally, for parts of my life. He wants to make it clear that not only was he there for my black belt, but he was *there*.

"Okay, okay, just making sure, old-timer! You know you forget shit."

"I don't fucking forget anything!"

"What did we eat for dinner last night?"

He pauses, then dodges the question, "You were talking about your fucking book guy."

I nod in victory. "Uh huh, that's what I thought. You still sneaking those Benadryl?"

He ignores the question. "All right, fine. I remember, but let's just tell the story for the record."

"What record?"

"The record, the fucking record, I dunno, we're off the freeway already! We'll be there in ten minutes."

I laugh at the exchange, but the mention of the Benadryl gives me a pang of anxiety. We have not really spoken much of the incident, although my mother and I had a conversation about it privately. The only solution is to be able to watch him around the clock. She works, and I own a school and live in my own house with the kids. I ponder a few options, some of which will take a big commitment. I have to think it through.

"Hey son, you still with me?"

"Sorry, the black belt. Okay . . ."

———•———

I was never in jiu-jitsu for a black belt. During my reign of terror as a brown belt, my only motivation was to get back to ADCC trials and avenge my loss. But, naturally, black comes after brown, and winning so many championships at brown belt gets a person thinking.

Every white belt is in a hurry to get their blue belt, and every blue is in a hurry to get their purple. But as the years tick by, the art makes a patient person out of you. Just like you learn to take your time passing and choking, you wait out the next belt as if it were an opponent on the mat. Eventually it will come to everyone who keeps training.

In a practical sense, I was at the black belt level. Everyone respected me as if I was a black belt. On any given day, I could defeat any black belt Renzo could throw at me. Not ten out of ten times; mind you, Renzo doesn't give black belts to the unexceptional. But I liked my chances against any of his guys.

The belt is special though. It's a symbol; it's a trophy. Some people say it doesn't matter, but those same people wear their black belt every time they train for a reason. And a black belt from Renzo Gracie and Ricardo Almeida is sort of like being first among equals. People that train under them don't say they are black belts; they say they are *Ricardo Almeida* black belts or *Renzo Gracie* black belts. When I lay in bed at night, I would dream first and foremost about winning ADCC. But in those dreams, I wore a black belt (okay, I wouldn't wear an actual belt at ADCC, but in my dreams I made it work somehow).

In early 2009, Ricardo told me in not so many words, that the time was close. It was too much of an open secret to try and surprise me. He told me he was proud of me, and so was Renzo, and that they wanted to have a special event for me the following week. I tried and failed to hold back a grin. Ricardo failed to hold his own in as well. It's a secret that only instructors know: the black belt promotion is as important to the teacher as to the student. Every student starts out as deadweight; some will eventually pull their own. But in every gym there is a core group that carries the brunt of the load. They do the teaching or win the medals, or both. I had been mentored along, like so many others, by Ricardo and his team. But now I was the guy other people looked to for guidance. I was also a soldier. I had spent the last two years flying the Renzo Gracie flag. I never competed under my own school name. I had even encouraged my students to compete as Ricardo Almeida fighters.

Ricardo picked me up on a Saturday morning and took me to a large building that used to be an armory outside of Jersey. Back then, the Renzo academy wasn't big enough to hold that many people. We pulled up to the nondescript building, in the back lot. I remember it was so empty that it felt like I was about to get whacked.

I wasn't, and when we entered the armory it felt like almost everyone I knew in my life was there. My mother and father, Renzo, all of their students, and all of my students. It was around one hundred people, all gathered there for me. In your lifetime, you rarely get to experience moments where so many people are gathered just for you, not because you're going to give them anything, but because they just want to be a part of your moment.

Renzo, full of his usual charisma, gave a proud speech totally off the cuff. As usual, he knew exactly what to say. With Renzo, his words always took a backseat to his spirit. I could feel from his smile, his laugh, the way he would put his hand on my shoulder that he was proud of me. For someone who had lost the ADCC trials for Team Renzo two years before, it felt good to hear Renzo tell a hundred people that he was proud to make me a black belt today. I knew Renzo never blamed me for what happened, but sometimes you just need to hear it.

Ricardo spoke next. He was different from Renzo. He couldn't make you laugh on cue, but he didn't try to be something he wasn't. If Renzo was the happy warrior, Ricardo was the intense one. At that time, Ricardo was fighting in the UFC, winning fights and slowly climbing the ladder. He had assembled a legendary team, including guys like Frankie Edgar, who was now being seriously considered as a contender for a UFC title shot.

At the end of their speeches, they both tied a black belt around my waist. People cheered; everyone wanted hugs and pictures. I felt happy, but, as always, something held me back. A hundred people had gathered just to see me succeed, people that cared about me and were happy for me. I went to bed that night, in my new house that I had bought. I had a black belt, I was a brown belt champion, I had money, I had friends.

But, as crazy as it sounds, I felt incredibly lonely.

CHAPTER 17

The night my father had his overdose, I left the hospital in the darkest place I had ever been.

I drive up to a hardware store, in a fog. There's no real plan; my hands just sort of turn the steering wheel until I come to a stop in front of it. My father's words from an hour ago ring in my head.

Please, my son gave me this.

Even as I browse the ropes, it still isn't real. More of a what-if kind of thing. It would need to be thick and not too long. I check a bag or two to see if any of them overtly state how much weight they can hold.

I ultimately buy two different kinds. As I check out, I eye the cashier for any sort of suspicion. He can give two shits about me; he hardly looks up from his register.

I can always put them in my closet, just keep them there as some sort of reminder, or option. I don't need to do anything. So I bought a rope. So what?

But fifteen minutes later, I'm driving around some trails near my house, eyeing a few trees. They would need to be tall, and strong. Maybe I would need a stool. Maybe I could climb the tree and then jump.

The logistics of it should scare me, but they don't. I wish they did. The truth is, I have trouble feeling fear. Not because I'm special, or tough, or brave. I think I'm some sort of sociopath. I glance down at my arm, seeing the bulging and shiny area of skin in the shape of a cross. I notice for the first time that I'm out of the car, the rope in my right hand, still in its package.

I walk for a long time, maybe an hour. I think over and over about my father somehow finding my body hanging limp from one of these trees. Something is in my heart, a feeling of desperation. A feeling that I can never make my father see how what he does hurts me. But maybe this, this could be it. I could die, to make my father understand. Day has become afternoon on the trail I'm walking. As the shadows on the trail get longer, my thoughts get darker. It's a cold day, one where the difference between the sunlight and the shadows feels like ten degrees. As I walk and feel my body shiver one moment and warm the next, my mind goes through a similar cycle. The reasons for my own death shift and morph in my mind. Resentment, martyrdom, hope, release, revenge, vindication. The disturbing realization that my own death would not stop, but likely accelerate, my father's addiction is also in the mix.

I think of my mother, the most amazing person in my life. The only person who can understand me, because she understands the way I was raised. I think for the first time about her finding my body or getting a phone call. Several possible futures for her appear to me, none of them good ones. Anything I do to hurt my father, her pain will be greater. My father can retreat into drugs and alcohol. My mother will not. She will shoulder the pain, keep working, and keep existing.

Who am I kidding? The person who will find my body will be one of the many kids that play in these trails. I imagine an eight-year-old seeing me purple and white and hearing the creak of a taut rope swaying back and forth.

I don't know which of these thoughts persuades me to return to the car, or all of them. But I do return, and then I do something absolutely crazy: I go to the evening jiu-jitsu class. I disturb even myself at how routine the night is. In fact, once we get into sparring, I forget completely the past few hours. It's a powerful lesson to me I remember to this day. For all you know, the guy you just spoke to could have been about to kill himself earlier in the day.

My dad is released from the hospital the next day. He says that everything will change. This time it will all be different. It won't.

I'm grateful that I've moved out, so I won't have to see him slide back into using.

———•———

Knock knock.

I'm pulled out of my dark memory by the sound of knuckles tapping impatiently on window. My father is standing there, done with his morning Methadone and ready to slide back into my truck, his requisite high for the day achieved. I mumble an apology for not noticing his approach, and we get back on the road. I'm broody and testy, having deeply contemplated the time I seriously considered suicide in my early twenties, and the fact that the man responsible for many of those urges is sitting next to me now. Not only is he still using, but now I'm helping him do it. I'll continue until the end of his life.

My father playfully teases about my absence of mind. He presses me to continue on with the story, because we're finally at the good part. Up until this point, I had been taking mostly Ls in my career, maybe even my life. But things were about to turn around for me. It's 2009 now, and ADCC trials are coming back around . . .

———•———

At this time I felt a terrible sense of momentum in my life. It was clear that all roads lead back to ADCC, back to the trials that I lost two years ago. I had done what I needed to do. I had gotten my brown belt and won most of the major tournaments in the world in a single year, including the No-Gi World Championship. I hadn't been given my black belt so much as I took it by force by beating the best brown belts in the world.

So when it came back around to the 2009 ADCC trials, it was pretty clear there would be no in-house tournament this year. I was the designated hitter on the team. There was no ceremony of anointing me; everyone just knew. It was everything I wanted and it terrified me at the same time. I knew that winning was the storybook ending, but I had lived in the real world enough to know that I could also lose.

There are people in this sport, sometimes called gym warriors, that acquire a reputation as someone who can beat anybody in the gym but nobody in the high pressure situations. I wasn't a gym warrior, I knew that. I had the medals to prove it on my wall. But those medals were brown belt medals. This was black belt, and not even just that—these were the best in the world. I had fought them once and lost quickly. If I lost a second time, I was afraid that the stereotype would stick. I couldn't let that happen. The image of losing in front of Renzo was still seared into my memory.

Pressure is a terrible thing, and to this day I've never had pressure on me like I did that summer. I was representing my own fledgling school, my teacher, and *his* teacher. There was no way to go but forward. Dropping out wasn't an option, losing wasn't an option. I had painted myself into a corner, maybe on purpose. I was confident, but everyone was confident. Everyone thought the universe was on their side. But skill would always matter, always be the main factor in a win or a loss. I knew this, and it wasn't comforting.

Nowadays ADCC trials are full media productions, streamed live and with the same quality as a world championship. But in 1999, we were in a high-school gym on the East Coast. There were also no fans, outside of maybe a few family members. Jiu-jitsu was not yet a spectator sport. Virtually everyone there was a competitor, which also meant that the guy to your left could well be Renzo Gracie or Marcelo Garcia. There were also few sponsors. I wore a Ricardo Almeida t-shirt and some baggy shorts. No one made any money; no one was looking to sell their instructionals.

My first opponent was named Azunna Anyanwu. He was a mountain of a man. I fought in the heavyweight division, and I was used to being undersized there. I was in an odd place with my size: too big to cut down my weight and too small to bully people. There was no tape or fight footage of Azunna; I went into it blind.

In the first few seconds, I could tell by the way he moved that he was not a pace pusher. Heavyweights often are not. He lumbered around in a low stance, probing with his hands every now and again. We did all the things that grapplers do when they know nothing about each other and the stakes are too high to be reckless. We fought for hand control, then for collar ties, then played with level changes. We didn't commit particularly hard to anything. It was more for information-gathering, to see if there was any low-hanging fruit in our reactions that either of us could exploit. ADCC matches last for up to twenty-four minutes, which is an eternity in grappling. The opening moves are critical to size up the basic skill level of your opponent, or just to see if you can provoke any reaction.

Ricardo was in my corner, mere feet from me. He wouldn't even have to yell instructions. He sat calmly on a chair. Ricardo was an excellent coach. He knew what each fighter needed in the moment. I needed to relax and pace myself. This was just the first match. Conservation of energy was everything. As the smaller man, getting Azunna down to that mat would take significant energy, so I had to be strategic. I also knew that, judging by his size, getting him underneath me would be a major step towards exhausting him.

As time went on, I began to get antsy. One of us needed to explode and get this thing going. I then made a critical mistake that Ricardo still makes fun of to this day. I turned to look behind me at Ricardo, taking my eyes off my opponent completely, to ask Ricardo a question,

"How much tim—"

Before I could finish the sentence, I felt about 250 pounds of force barrel into my stomach. Azunna had seen his shot and didn't waste it. With my eyes not on him, he dropped down for a blast double, launching me into the air and down on the mat. I had given him a free takedown, and now I had a grappler of greater size and possibly equal skill on top of me. I looked up and saw Ricardo, mere feet from my face. His face showed barely contained frustration, no doubt at his star student's mistake. I swore I wouldn't lose in front of him like I lost in front of Renzo.

The ref broke us up and moved us back to the center of the mat, although we kept our position with me on the bottom. It was the few seconds I needed to reset my focus. I was still primarily a guard player. I was dangerous on the bottom, perhaps the most dangerous. I had felt Azunna's game for only a few seconds, but I knew that I had something for him. I quickly opened my guard and moved into half guard, my favorite position. I used a knee shield to keep him at bay and waited to see what his counter was from here. He tried repeatedly to perform the same guard pass, and I knew I had the upper hand. He wasn't cycling through tactics. I needed to wait him out. The clock burned down, getting into the final minutes of the match now. Eventually, he gave me what I wanted, leaning too far into me, allowing for me to underhook a leg and initiate a sweep, which I finished to get on top of him. I stole a cautious glance at the judges' table. I has been awarded two points for the sweep, and the match had just two minutes left. I made all the use I could of my couple hundred pounds, buying myself another minute or so of top control. Azunna was fighting with desperation now, knowing that he had to score or submit. The time for caution was over. He made a reckless move and turned his back to me in a bid to get back to his feet. It paid off, and he sprang to his feet, turned around, and charged me like a bull. I dodged and circled, using my light feet to my advantage. He charged again, practically stumbling off the mat this time. I knew he didn't have much left. He lowered his stance again and set his jaw for one last, herculean effort.

And I'm sure it would have been a good one, but I'll never know for sure. At that moment the bell rang. The match was over. I had won by a mere two points to zero (due to the somewhat convoluted rule structure of ADCC, he scored no points for his takedown).

I didn't yell, take my shirt off, or point towards the heavens. It was just the first round, nothing to celebrate. I looked over my shoulder to sneak a grin at Ricardo for my near-fatal mistake of asking him about the match time. When I did, my smile faded. Ricardo had left to go to another match. He hadn't even seen me finish.

It was only the first match.

———•———

"Tree two foa you Tom! Is tree two foa you! Less go!"

Ricardo's voice rings in my ear from across the gym. There is a lot of crosstalk between my team and my opponent's, as his own coaches scream with urgency. They are just as invested as their fighter; some of them crouch and try to get eye level, others slap their knees or hit their chairs with every word. My coach shouts with his thick Brazilian accent, intermixed with a few Jersey ones. It's madness. I can't always even distinguish between advice for me and advice for him.

No one really needs to shout, because the gym I am fighting in is virtually silent as the onlookers watch my match and only my match. It's the only one taking place. And yet, now is the time to get animated, because this is the ADCC North American Trials Finals Match. The last match of the day, and the only match that really matters. There are no silver medals in the trials. You either win and punch your ticket to the championships in Barcelona, Spain, or you go home to tell people about how you fought in the trials one time. And, as Ricardo just said, I'm up three points to two.

Getting those three points had taken over twenty minutes of grappling. Before that, it had taken another ten-minute match against another heavyweight, and before that there was Azunna Anyanwu. Before that was the last two years of my life. None of it would matter unless I could maintain my one-point lead for the next six minutes.

As this thought briefly crossed my mind, Ricardo snapped me out of it again,

"Less keepa de offense, keepa de offense!"

He's right. My opponent is the largest heavyweight I have ever fought. He's 260 pounds of pure muscle, not like most heavyweights back then who had quite a bit of body fat. I've seen him before at tournaments. He always makes the podium. He's bigger, stronger, and at least as skilled as me, fighting his own way to the finals. And right now, he's on top and attacking relentlessly. We are in overtime, meaning points are in effect. He is down one point but in a strong position to get it, having already passed into my half guard.

He is also considerably less tired than me. Perhaps he had easier matches, or just so didn't expend much energy. He sees me wiping sweat from my eyes, and he knows that his window to score is now.

My saving grace is that I have a good half guard, and a nearly unpassable guard (my guard had never been passed in brown belt competition). I don't know much about him technically, but as I attack his legs from the bottom of half guard, I feel his body reacting as if he doesn't quite know how to proceed. He resorts to simply pushing me away and trying to pin my legs in vain to the ground. I see him probing my defenses, mentally alternating attacks to find a weak spot. But as he begins to repeat tactics that he's already tried, I know that he is out of ideas. I'm the current point leader, which means he must attack to win. I must attack as well, but more to keep him mentally occupied and distracted from the real problem of passing my guard.

"Haffway Tom!" yells Ricardo, indicating five minutes left.

My opponent's coaches bark instructions at him, urging him to make something happen. He wisely determines that he doesn't have time to crack the riddle of my half guard, and he begins to set up for a footlock. I recognize it and scoop up control of his neck to check it. Without the ability to separate his body from mine, his footlock is doomed to failure. But, in a pivotal error, he sits back for it anyways.

I seize on his mistake, using my neck control to catch a ride as he sits back, landing me on top. Even better, his enormous size pulls me straight to my feet, where his leg attack is negated and I have now reversed the position. The referee waits a few seconds, then raises his hand to award me points.

His corner goes ballistic now. The math just got harder for them. He needs not one but two scoring moves now to pull ahead, or he can submit me and the match is over, along with the last two years of my life.

I'm not thinking about that, though. I'm fully in the moment again. Although I have taken top position, it's precarious. His massive tree-trunk legs are entangled with my own, and if I am not careful, I will easily get tipped over. We fight a small battle for control of my hips, where I need to fend off his feet while resisting the urge to move my feet. If I lift a foot off the ground even an inch, he will off-balance me and likely footlock me within seconds. I patently clear his leg and collapse on him, killing any chance of a sweep.

The win is almost in the bag now, but as my mind processes this, it almost gives my body an invisible signal to let up. A wave of exhaustion hits me as I heave breaths so deep it feels like I am choking on my own oxygen. What I need to do is secure my new position on top in his half guard, but I feel sluggish. Ricardo pleads with me to get an underhook and get chest to chest on my opponent. While I hear him, my body doesn't respond. I lose the space that I need to pin him down on the mat, and with a powerful scoot backwards he escapes and gets back to his feet.

I stand up and take a deep breath. Jiu-jitsu is a game of momentum. If you let someone score a small victory, you'd better make sure they don't score a second or third. The momentum may have shifted in his favor again, and he knew it. He had no doubt spent precious blood and sweat to get here too, and I knew he would dig deep now to seize on his chance.

Ricardo, a skilled tactician, saw this and immediately yelled at me to attack for a takedown. This time, I followed his instructions immediately. I shot just about the worst takedown of my life, the best I could do under the circumstances. I was countered and snapped down to the mats immediately. My opponent smelled blood and had a surge of energy. He spun around to my back, which I narrowly avoided by trapping him back into half guard. I saw he had his hand too low and snapped my legs up for a triangle. The crowd erupted, but I knew that I didn't have it and retreated back to half guard.

I had lost track of the points, but Ricardo yelled that somehow I was up now by a single point. I didn't know how much time was left, but I knew it couldn't be much. Scoring even a single point is hard in this format, let alone after a day of fighting and more than twenty minutes into a match. I've never believed in stalling, but I do believe in being smart. The truth was, it was *his* turn to take risks if he wanted to win. A feeling of desperation had set into his motions. He didn't have the luxury of time to slowly crack my defenses. He tried to knee-slice pass, then went to a double-under pass, then a standing pass. With each attempt, he would abandon it if it did not get results within seconds. A confidence set in: I realized that this person had nothing for me. He knew it too; he was just going through the motions now. After all, he couldn't give up.

Finally, he stood up and for a brief second put his hands on his hips in exhaustion. From my back, I motioned him in emphatically. He heaved a big breath, dropped his hand, and dropped back down to resume. But as far as I was concerned, the match was over. I had broken him.

Long after the bell rang and I had my hand raised, I reflected that I had won the fight the same way I had accomplished most things in my life: resilience. I didn't win via a flash submission or a quick finish. I grinded it out over nearly half an hour of grappling. It was the kind of win I liked the most. There was no doubt, no questioning whether it was luck or "having a good day." It was a definitive win, a true win. A Tom DeBlass win.

"Must've felt so good to finally get that win."

I take a moment before saying, "Yeaaaah, I think it felt good."

Dad curls his lips in curiosity. "You *think* that it did?"

"No, it definitely did."

"Well, what did you do that night?"

I tilt my head, trying to think and focus on the road.

"I . . . I don't know. I'm sure we celebrated, but I don't really remember."

My Dad looks at me and nods his head in almost a mocky way. "Huh. Biggest win of your life, huh?"

"Well, the trials just gets you into ADCC, like the championships. That's what the ultimate goal was. I didn't win those."

"But winning the trials is super hard, right?"

"Yeah, the North American Trials are, like, such a big deal to win."

"So were you happy?"

"It was a big accomplishment for sure."

"Were you happy?"

I squirm a bit in my seat, "I was happy, yeah. I was focused. I remember training on Monday for the championship."

We pull up to the house. Dad opens the door, looks back, and says, "Seems like you weren't happy."

He says it with a little grin on his face, and I smile back. I roll down my window and begin my twenty-minute drive to Ocean County Jiu-jitsu.

I think about what he said. It wasn't that I wasn't happy. Maybe I just didn't stop to let myself be happy for more than two goddamn hours. As soon as I got home, my thoughts had turned to the next thing. The next tournament. The next win.

CHAPTER 18

Every other year, all trials winners advance to the ADCC champion-ships. In addition, a small group of competitors are invited without having to compete in the trials. Those invited are considered the undisputed best in the world, so much so that they don't need to win the trials. The trials is more of a mechanism to produce wildcards, relative unknowns that can surprise. That was me in the 2009 cham-pionships. ADCC Championships in 2009 was widely considered to have the best competitors in a generation. Names like Andre Galvao, Fabricio Werdum, Roberto Abreu, and Saulo Ribeiro. All in my division.

The tournament was held in Barcelona, Spain. Traveling overseas for a tournament adds a dimension of stress. Most competitors will tell you that the slow buildup before competing is the worst. Most of us would rather take a fight on a few days' notice, at least mentally. Organizing travel in a foreign country throws everyone off. The food is different, the language is different, and the times are different.

I had competed against big names, but nowhere near this. My sixteen-man division was a murderers' row of names: future Hall of Famers and UFC champions. I wanted to win, and I planned to win. But I tried not to think about some of the names in my division. Some of my opponents had literally never had their guards passed, or never been submitted. Whoever won, this division could fairly be called the best in the world.

My first match was against Roberto "Cyborg" Abreu, named Cyborg because of a serious car accident that left glass in his left arm. The Brazilian heavyweight was known for his innovative guard game, which he had styled the "tornado guard." I had been following him most of my career. I remember watching him have an all-out war at the world championships when I was still a brown belt in 2007. In our division, more than a few had labeled him the favorite.

As often happens when you grapple on the very highest levels, our match came down to a game of inches. Someone has to win, but sometimes two grapplers can be so close that declaring a winner becomes almost subjective. Towards the end of our match I was penalized for inactivity and given a negative point. The match ended zero to negative one for Cyborg. It was a bitter way to lose, made worse by what happened next. After the match, the official told me that they thought I was Cyborg. The penalty was meant for him.

There was no judges' review, no instant replay, and no appeal process. They fucked up, pure and simple. Was I upset? Yes, but not enough to make a big deal. The truth was, even the winner couldn't really hold their head too high winning in a match with no significant action.

The other hard truth was that my match with Cyborg was only the first round. Could I have won the whole sixteen-man tournament? Maybe, but even Cyborg was knocked off in the finals.

I had been invited to fight in the absolute division, and my first match was against Andre Galvao. Galvao was not yet quite in the prime of his career; he would take the bronze in this ADCC and go on to become the most successful ADCC champion of all time in terms of wins. We fought an exciting fight. Before points, he swept me early and I swept him back. He took my back, but I escaped and attempted a footlock. It was not successful, and we finished the match with him up by three points.

It was a ceiling moment in my career. I left Spain with little to show. I had struck out in my only two matches. True, they were against two of the best. But then again, everyone was the best here.

As I took the flight home, I felt defeated. I had made it to the highest levels and hit a wall. I had lost my first matches, but I wondered if I could have won *any* of the matches. And yet, a part of me held hope. I had lost my matches, but hadn't been outclassed. No submissions, not even my guard was passed. I fought Cyborg to a standstill, who would go on to become one of the greats.

One of the great gifts and curses of competitors is their ability to do what I just described. They can always talk themselves into one more chance. Once my depression over the losses faded, I returned to the gym ready to do it all again. Next time would be different. I wouldn't be starstruck, I wouldn't be jet-lagged, I wouldn't be injured.

Next time would be different.

CHAPTER 19

I tap my foot impatiently and look at my phone for the third time. I've texted twice, the same text as always

Here.

Sometimes Dad is running late, I tell myself. Especially if Mom has gone off to work early, which she has this morning. I don't want to overreact. He hates when I do that—rush in the house in panic, worried about him. I'll look like an idiot. So I decide to give him another minute. After about 20 seconds, my gut gets the better of me.

He hears the door open and calls out immediately. I find him at the foot of the stairs, just sitting there. He gives an impatient sigh and mutters something under his breath.

"Dad, you okay?" I choke a little as the words come out, not really prepared for all the things he might say.

He waves his hand in frustration, "I just lost my footing for a second there." He rubs his knee with one hand, hoping I'll put two and two together. I do: My Dad fell and he can't get up.

His eyes follow me as I look from his knee up to the stairs and back down to him. He sees the look of recognition in my eyes and nods in the affirmative. Every man has dignity, and in that moment I know that it's important to my father that I not spell it out. However long he's been sitting here, it's been long enough to think about the hundred implications of him possibly not being able to traverse the stairs in his house. The house he's lived in for forty years. The house I grew up in.

"Ah, so you missed a step, huh?" I force a casual tone in my voice.

"You know, ever since your mother put the carpet in . . ." His voice trails off. That carpet was put in twenty years ago. But I take the out he just gave himself and decide to sit next to him for a minute.

"Well, hey, let's get your thoughts together, and then we'll get you up. Can I see the leg?"

"Ahh, it's fine."

"Then there won't be much to see, huh?"

He looks at me, knowing that he's stuck. He mutters a curse word and pulls up his grey sweats. I resist the urge to diagnose the knee on the spot, something I'm accustomed to, being that I run a jiu-jitsu academy. I would normally feel it, test the range of motion and such. But the goal is to calm him down right now. A quick look at the leg shows a bruise coloring up, which tells me nothing in particular, but maybe it's a good sign that it's muscular and not something with the bone.

"How long you been sitting here?"

He rubs his chin like the question has multiple possible answers, and eventually settles on, "Twenty minutes, maybe more."

I nod impassively. That's not good. We spend a minute or two reviewing his morning to distract ourselves. He tells me what he ate for breakfast, when he got in the shower, and the like. He finally arrives to the moment he fell, making it clear that he could have gotten to his feet at any time but thought it might be best to sit for a second. I don't press him for why, then, he didn't get up to retrieve his phone when he knew I would soon be arriving. Instead, I mention that I had been thinking of spending more time with him soon. His ears prick up at this, and I go on to propose that maybe I could spend the days with him when Mom is working.

"You would want to take your old room, then?"

"Yeah, sure. I mean, maybe we could even do better than that."

He raises an eyebrow. "What do you mean by that?"

We settle on the old "we'll think about it and talk later." But as I help him get to the car, I feel the limp on his leg, the frailness of his body. My father has lost close to thirty pounds in the last five years. I had wondered about it, perhaps not enough. Now, I wondered every hour I wasn't with him if he was sneaking out to go get more Benadryl, or something worse. He feels his body changing too, and we both realize in that moment, without words, that it's going to happen. I will move back in with my parents to be close and watch out for them. They would do the same for me, and they basically have in other ways. We've always been a tight-knit family. No one can understand what we've been through, what we've endured. We never talked about what was going on with us to outsiders. And everybody that wasn't us was an outsider.

I get him in the car, and we take off. I briefly consider skipping the clinic on account of the state that I found him in. But I quickly remember that it's not an option. My father can go a day or two without methadone at best. At his age and health, even that might kill him.

As we drive, we continue the story where we left off. It's become a natural ritual, even if today there are a hundred other things on our minds as I retell the fallout of ADCC 2009.

Victory, like all highs, is temporary. At Team Renzo Gracie, even more so. I had won the trials but had not even cleared the first round of the championships. In fact, I hadn't even scored a point.

Still, the trials win meant I was one of the best grapplers in the world, objectively. But back home, the world kept moving forward. There was almost immediately talk of the next fight, the next tournament. Ricardo was on a three-fight win streak, preparing for the biggest fight of his life against Matt Hughes. Another Ricardo Almeida student, Frankie Edgar, had gone from sacrificial lamb for all-time great B.J. Penn to the reigning lightweight champion and was about to do it again in a rematch.

Up the road at Renzo's, his academy had become a tourism destination. On any given day, it was a Who's Who of celebrities on the mats, people coming to town for access to skilled training partners and teachers—the most famous of whom was Georges St-Pierre, who lauded his training under John Danaher as a sort of secret weapon, causing hundreds of other fighters to make the Renzo academy a sort of pilgrimage each year. Renzo welcomed the visitors and the elevated status of the gym. The tradeoff was that longtime Renzo students such as myself were cautious, aware that today's visitors would be tomorrow's rivals. We were wary of sharing too many Renzo secrets.

The Renzo team itself had become more akin to medieval clans, united by loyalty to Renzo but always tested. Team Renzo, Team Almeida, and Team Serra had emerged as the three major flag-bearers for Renzo Gracie. All three teams were very good, often fielding athletes and fighters at the same tournaments. They also had UFC fighters. In the UFC, declining to fight teammates was perilous; it was an easy way to fall out of grace with the matchmakers. With a typical division having only twenty-five or so names, and only four to six divisions in those times, it was inevitable that teammates would have to fight eventually.

It was a delicate balance, and lesser men would not have upheld it. How Renzo did it was a riddle. He didn't exactly rule with an iron fist. He was as much a teammate as an instructor. But his laid-back approach was commanding nonetheless. Loyalty was simply baked into his family. He never had to explicitly tell us how to behave, but we just knew what was acceptable and what wasn't. The few times I saw Renzo get angry with people, it was terrifying. And he was considered *the nice one* amongst his brothers.

I knew I was a part of the best team in the world, because despite winning the ADCC trials I was still on the JV team at Ricardo's. Hell, I probably would have been even if I had won the championship. The truth was, all roads led back to MMA. Financially, it was the only option for a livable income at that time. You could win every jiu-jitsu title in the world and be broke, but a starter contract with the UFC guaranteed $10,000 just to show, and another $10,000 to win. It also provided health insurance, which was easily worth $50,000 a year. MMA athletes are virtually uninsurable otherwise.

But, truthfully, it was more the desire to compete that compelled me to make the call. Money was coming in from my academy in Oceanside. I had bought a house for the first time in my life. But training at Ricardo's meant you had to train MMA regularly to help teammates prepare for their own fights. Eventually, you ask yourself why you're training like an MMA fighter without at least giving it a shot.

As a known name from a major camp, it wasn't hard to get into MMA. Ricardo had Dana White's cell phone number. But I knew that you only get one chance in the UFC, which was cutting any fighter that went on a three-fight losing streak. Grapplers were often more likely to get that phone call. The UFC was about to hit the big time; rumors of a new TV deal with a major network were flying around. They didn't have room for bad fighters, but they had less room for boring ones.

I needed to get a record under my belt, a good one. That meant taking my time and fighting at my level. I was a world-class grappler, but I was still developing my striking every day at the gym. I was leaps and bounds better than my last MMA fight, which had been years earlier at this point. Still, everyone had seen what an elite striker could do to an elite grappler who couldn't score a takedown.

Ring of Combat was the largest promoter on the East Coast at that time. They were sometimes a feeder organization for large promotions, but they sometimes competed directly, signing talented athletes and bringing them along to become champions. They had broadcast rights in several East Coast markets. Essentially, they were the biggest stage you could fight on without a professional record, and that's where I made my start.

The transition from grappler to MMA fighter wasn't much of a transition. Ricardo Almeida had become a full-fledged MMA team, so much so that even Renzo and his students would travel to Ricardo's for MMA training. I was training MMA regularly.

It speaks to how much experience I had acquired that my first few fights in the cage weren't that big a deal. I fought three times in the first year, all within six months. All were victories. The next year, 2011, I fought another three times. One of those was a submission victory against a former UFC fighter. My opponents began to get better and better. They were almost always bigger than me. I was known as a small light heavyweight.

The competition got stiffer. The matches became more tactical, requiring more adjustments each time. In the beginning, my opponents were simply overmatched by my grappling and sometimes my striking. It didn't matter where the match went; I was going to be fine. But later on, it became more of an equation. If the match goes in this direction, I win. If it goes another direction, I could very well lose.

The wins kept coming. By the end of 2011, I was offered the light heavyweight title against Mike Stewart. I overwhelmed him in the first round for a TKO victory. In an odd way, even winning the title isn't particularly noteworthy in my head all these years later.

I'll tell you what is noteworthy: my first title defense in ROC. It was one of the hardest MMA fights of my professional career. My opponent was Davit Tkeshelashvili. He was straight out of Rocky IV. He was Mirko Cro Cop, Fedor Emelianenko, and Khabib Nurmagomedov, all rolled into one. A heavyweight that cut down to 205, built like a Greek sculpture, and with the disposition of a stoic samurai. He was from the Republic of Georgia and had been some sort of special forces solider in a former life. At Team Renzo, where geography and geopolitics wasn't our strong suit, we all considered him Russian. At the time, the most feared fighter on the planet, Fedor Emelianenko, was Russian. Davit was similar in that he rarely spoke or expressed much in the way of emotion.

By this time, I was a seasoned fighter. No fight was ever easy, but no fight was to-the-death either. All that changed with Davit. He was the toughest man I fought up until that time. My philosophy on fighting was that you have to be better somewhere. If he has better wrestling, then you need to be better at striking and jiu-jitsu. If he has better striking, you need to have better wrestling. Davit was one of the first fighters I encountered that, one, had very little footage or intel on his style. Two, from what we *could* find out about him, he seemed decent everywhere. His size was a particular concern. He was a heavyweight in all but name only, but a rare breed of heavyweight. He wasn't fat but muscular. He could shrink down to 205 pounds, make the weight for the fight, and then balloon back up to 245 pounds overnight.

We did have one advantage, though: he seemed slow. He moved with the lumbering pace of a man whose natural weight was probably 275 pounds. We had found videos of him working out. He could go hard and long but not particularly fast. It was enough to build a basic game plan from. I was going to push the pace, make him move around the cage, and never let him set his feet. No rock 'em sock 'em robots.

The fight, of course, didn't pan out perfectly. It was the nightmare scenario: all the things we were worried about Davit doing well, he did. But then he surprised us with other skills we didn't anticipate. For one, he was a skilled wrestler after all. He shot for power takedowns, moved to pass my guard, and even had me in turtle at one point.

Beyond that, his punches were all thrown with one million percent power. A clean hit would have probably decapitated me. When you literally feel the air blown in your eyes from a punch that misses you by an inch, it's a terrifying thing.

As the fight progressed, a few things became apparent. Davit was a heavy hitter but not a particularly technical striker. I was able to dart in and out, peppering him with punches. He also was a good wrestler but didn't have much for me on the ground. I swept him from half guard at a critical point in the fight.

Midway through the second round, I felt his energy change. He was getting tired. His hands got lower, his kicks felt like nothing. He would feign punches but not commit to them. I had him.

As the third round opened up, he gave one last, explosive shot. I hurled my heels back and dropped my weight like I was dodging a car. I sprawled on top of him and wasted no time spinning to his back. I felt all the invisible indicators of a man who had fired his last bullet, and I took the strength I had left and poured it on. Ricardo yelled at me to pace myself for the round, so I did. Not a barrage of punches, but constant and consistent ones. I stayed on top and rode out the rest of the round. In the end, there was no question who had won.

But all of that, the whole story, wasn't what made it memorable. That happened after the fight. In the cage, hands were raised and my name was read to the crowd. I was the hometown hero, and, given that my opponent was foreign born, there were more than a few chants of "U.S.A.!" going around.

Davit's corner took it all in stride. He looked at the canvas stoically as the decision was read. He shook my hand, unable to say much in English but still able to exchange a look and a nod that conveyed as much respect and professionalism as any words would have. I shook hands with his modest team. Each of them looked angry at the loss, but not necessarily at me personally.

One of the men in his team approached me in the ring. He looked older than the rest. He rattled off words in another language as he approached with his hands out. He clasped my cheeks with them. I felt the roughness of his hands, hands that had clearly worked, rough with calluses. He continued to talk to me. While I could only study his face, I had two realizations. The first was that he was emotional and saying something from the heart. The second was that he was Davit's father.

A younger man appeared at his side and addressed me. "He says you fought well, you gave his son the fight you both deserved."The old man had spoken far too long for that to be the whole of it, but I accepted his words and nodded. I placed my hands at my side and bowed to him, a universal symbol of respect.

The old man reached into his collar and fished a silver necklace out of his shirt. After some fidgeting, he revealed a pair of dog tags in his hand. They looked very old; the silver had turned a dull grey. He removed them from his neck and placed them in my palm, which still had my sweaty MMA gloves in them. I started to shake my head politely, but he closed my fist and pushed the hand to my chest. He clasped both of his hands over mine so that I held the tags tightly.

"He wants you to have it," the other man said, raising an eyebrow at the old man as if he couldn't believe it himself. "It is . . . special to him."

I did not have the energy to say much. I was still coming off of five rounds of intense combat. The soreness would set in soon, the intense fatigue. Then maybe the headaches. I leaned in close and touched my forehead to his.

"Thank you." I said. I looked in his eyes and saw tears. I don't fully understand all of it, what the story was with the tags or the man. But that night, we exchanged something special. It was a man and a father. A father who loved his son, so much that maybe he loved any man who could bring him down like I had. I never saw any of them again, but I feel in my heart that old man is in heaven, waiting for us.

"So that's it, isn't it?"

My father motions to the tags hanging abovemy dashboard. They hang unimpressively, just old lumps of metal. I often think about how it was created halfway across the world maybe as much as a hundred years ago, after which it went on an improbable journey that ultimately landed it in my truck in New Jersey.

"Yeah, there it is." I say, using a tone that masks my true feelings toward it. Conflicted feelings, for some reason. I love and hate those tags.

"Must've been important to you," Dad pries.

"Yeah, I guess."

A brief pause, but he won't let it go.

"Why is it so important?"

"Well, it's, it's—I dunno, it was just touching, you know? He had trained his son, been at all his fights. It was just this symbol of respect. I was honored, I guess."

My Dad goes quiet then says softly, "You know, I came to as many as I could."

"I know, dude, you were at nearly all of them. It's not about that at all. It was just nice. Don't read into it."

Even as I say the words, I wonder if it's more. If maybe my father is on to something. Was Davit Tkeshelashvili's father something I wanted in my relationship with my own father? At least, back then? Things had gotten so much better with him as we got older. But you can't change the past. My father wasn't there that night. I had searched the crowd for his face, listened to his voice. But he wasn't anywhere to be found.

CHAPTER 20

I often measure success not by how much money you have, but what you do with it. From the time I was a kid, I always wanted a pool. It wasn't uncommon in Jersey when I grew up, but it had gotten more expensive to have one. When you're a kid, it's required to have at least one friend with a pool. It made you just a little bit more in demand by default.

When you become a parent, you make it your goal to *be* the one with the pool. This is mainly so that you can keep an eye on your kids by making sure their friends come to your house, where you can check everyone out.

But also, it's just plain fun.

I sit in my backyard watching Isabelle launch herself off a rock into our family pool. She lets out a scream of pure joy before disappearing beneath the water. She climbs out, and my father and I immediately begin egging her on that her splash could have been even bigger if she were even trying. She argues playfully, then dives in to show off her handstands.

My father and I sit shirtless in the sun, enjoying the New Jersey heat. I like spending time with him. We talk about everything, but we mainly bond over the love of my kids.

The Story usually pauses on the weekends, but every now and again it continues organically. Today is one of those days.

"When do we get to the UFC?"

"I guess we could talk about that. There's so much more Ring of Combat stuff. You know, I was their champion in two divisions."

"Yeah, yeah, you were a killer. Seven and one, right?"

"Seven and zero, Pops. I never lost."

"But that first fight—"

"That was an amateur fight, didn't go on my record."

"Ah, okay. So did they roll out the red carpet for you in the UFC?"

"I wish. No, I was a short-notice replacement. I'll never forget the day I got the call." I look around and realize the irony, "In fact, I was sitting right here, right in this spot. On a day kind of like today."

"No shit?" says my Dad.

"Yeah, with an ice pad on my foot."

"Hey Tom, it's Ali."

I was a little annoyed to hear from my manager. I was on vacation, enjoying a Corona and trying not to think about fighting for a little while.

"Dude, what are you doing?" I say half jokingly. I'm referring to the specific instructions I gave him not to call me.

"You're gonna wanna hear this Tom. We got an offer. This is a big one. Are you sitting down?"

I look at my feet, reclined on a chair. The ice pack on my right one feels good in the heat, but other than that I hate it.

"Is that a joke?"

"Oh right, the ankle, yeah." Ali laughs it off, then tries to salvage it with a bad joke of some sort.

"Hey, trust me, you won't be laughing, er, I, we'll *both* be laughing after you hear—okay, let me tee this up for you. So I get a call—"

"Dude, four weeks, that's what the doctor said. No intense activity for four weeks. That means you can wait until I get back from—"

"Oh no, Tommy. No no no no. Let me stop you right there. This call, Tommy, you're gonna wanna hear them out."

Ring of Combat always did this, offering me the next fight before I was even ready. I had barely pulled out of the last one a week ago, and they were already trying to rebook it or give me someone new.

I sigh impatiently. I was having a pleasant afternoon on my patio. No shirt, no shoes, and enough alcohol to have just about no problems. Just the sound of Ali's voice makes me think of the dim lighting of his office, where he pushes his chair around to dig through papers and find the next bout agreement. I don't want to be there right now, physically or mentally.

"Tommy! Did you hear me, man?"

I snap out of my thoughts to realize Ali never stopped talking, "I, uh, yeah, just say it again."

"I'm saying it has to be tonight; I need to call them back with a yes or no on this. You don't keep this guy waiting."

"Listen, tell them I'm on vacation and the belt's not going anywhere for a few weeks, so they can—"

"The belt?! No, Tommy, this isn't ROC I'm talking about here. We're talking about the big show."

I lean up in my chair. The ice pack slides off my foot and falls to the ground, practically sizzling when it hits the hot surface.

"Wait, what? You're not talking about Ring of Combat?"

"Tommy, listen again: Joe Silva expects a callback in the next hour. If you say yes, I gotta get you on a flight back home and get you back in the gym."

My head is spinning now. "So the UFC? *That* Joe Silva?"

"Yeah, that's the only Joe Silva, the UFC matchmaker."

"And what's the match?"

"Cyrille Diabaté."

I know the name, but only vaguely. Striker, European of some sort. It's finally happening. I look at my ankle, more determined than ever to heal it. Even if the UFC wants me in a month, I can make it work.

"Tom, there's more." He says it like it's not good. "They need you in the Sweden card."

"Sweden? That card is in like three weeks."

"Tommy, it's in twelve days."

I take a long pause, understanding that I am ultimately going to say yes.

Ali knows this too, but maybe for a brief moment he thinks I might say no.

"Tommy, this is it."

Behind that sentence are a hundred unsaid implications. When the UFC calls, you say yes. If you don't, they go to the next name on the list, and your name may not come up next time. At this level, MMA was filled with divas that would play a hundred mind games to get a better fight, on a better card, for more money. I wasn't one of those divas, but no one knew that about me yet. They didn't know whether I was injured or just looking for a way out of a short-notice fight. A hundred men would fill my spot without a second thought if my manager didn't pick up that phone and say yes within the hour.

"Okay, Ali, call him back and tell him to get me the contract."

"Beautiful, beautiful. That's the right call, Tommy. The right call. How soon can you be in my office? I'll have the contract ready for you."

"Just fax it to the gym, I'm going straight—"

In mid-sentence, I feel a sharp pain as I stand up on my lounge chair and put weight on my ankle. I take a sharp breath. Twelve days.

"Hey, you okay, Tommy? You cut out there."

"Just fax me the contract."

CHAPTER 21

You never really get sleep the night of your fight. If you win, you're in for a night of partying, very likely to result in being dragged to an airport the next morning with a blurry memory of the evening.

If you lose, you will likely spend your night in a hospital, where your team sits with you in silence for a few hours, and your only companions for the evening are doctors who have little respect or awareness of what you just went through.

For a brief second, I am not quite sure which one I am. Am I hung over, in a strange room with minor bumps and cuts? Or am I lying in a hospital bed, beaten within an inch of my life? As the seconds tick by, the answer is clear. I can't breathe through my nose right, I can't open my eyes all the way. Just trying is painful, very painful.

My eyes come into focus enough for me to recognize the warm colors of a hotel room. I automatically move to get up. My whole body is sore, but it's my face that really hurts. I stand up, and my vision blurs immediately. I try to take a step, but I might as well be floating. I lose all sense of up or down, then feel the dull thud of hitting the carpet, accompanied by crashing glass and plastic that I hit on my way down. I lie on the floor for a second.

Despite waking in a hotel room, I remember now that it's only because I told the doctor I was fine. Ricardo drove me back to the hotel. In the three or so odd hours that I was able to sleep, the fight was on replay in my head. Some key memories stand out each time; others pop in and out as you forget moments and remember them suddenly.

I had an excellent first round, about as good as you could have. I scored a takedown early, worked past his guard, was isolating an arm. He managed to escape, and I got a second takedown. Surging with confidence, I repeated the process.

In the second round, I went right back to work, another take-down, and an even faster guard pass this time. Ricardo warned me not to separate myself too much in side control. That's how he had escaped last time, and it's how he did it again in the second round.

It was then that I began to feel the effects of not having a train-ing camp. When a fighter "gasses," it doesn't happen over time. It's more like someone flips a switch. One minute you're fine, and the next your body just deflates like a balloon. I think after Cyrille got back to his feet, my body in some mechanical way calculated the amount of energy it would need to score another takedown, another guard pass, and so on. That energy wasn't available, and from that moment on Cyrille came roaring back. Without the fear of an explosive takedown, the champion kickboxer in him came out. The long arms and legs of the Frenchman beat me back into a comfortable range and kept me there with hit after hit. I lost the second half of the second round, and everyone knew I would lose the third, barring a miracle.

Between rounds, Ricardo tells me to suck it up. It's like telling a car to keep going without gas. Heart and grit are important, but they can't fill your lungs with oxygen. I return to the cage in the third round fully aware that I'm about to get the ass-kicking of a lifetime.

It's the loneliest feeling in the world when the horn sounds and you watch your cornermen, camera crew, medics, everyone leave the cage. You hear someone latch the cage door shut. It's just me and an opponent who is fresher. A trained fighter, with zero empathy. I know I can't win, but I'm not tapping or covering up. I bite down on the mouthpiece and walk to the center of the octagon.

A chiming sound lurches me out of my thoughts. I'm standing in the hotel kitchen, holding a glass of water. The tap is running, I think it has been for a long time. I feel dizzy again. I look to my left, into the bedroom where I had collapsed. I don't know how long ago it was. I don't remember getting up or coming in here.

The chiming returns, and I reach into my pocket to pull out my phone. I smell sweat, and my hands are sticky. I realize I am wearing the same clothes I changed into after last night's fight.

I open my phone to see a text message from one of Ricardo's brothers:

Tough loss brother but you fight your heart out and never give up. Now it's time to move onto other things in your life. You don't need to fight anymore.

I stare at the text for awhile. I forgot a lot of things that happened that morning, but I'll never forget that text message. I don't know what the intention was, if he was some sort of genius of reverse psychology. But I know that the moment I saw it, I knew that I couldn't stop fighting. You could have put a million dollars in that kitchen sink, and I wouldn't have taken it over the dream of proving him wrong.

The text was, ultimately, the first of hundreds of comments made to me or at me about how I should quit. Ninety-nine percent of which were made out of earshot, online and in forums. It was a rude introduction to how, the moment you are on someone's television, you cease to become a real person. You're a character, there for someone's entertainment. You're just another extra in a movie. Your misfortune is equally as entertaining as your fortune.

I did not enjoy my trip to Sweden, to say the least. I spent the next day practically locked in a hotel room before a long flight home. I had been chewed up by Diabaté's leg kicks, and I hobbled around the hotel and, later, the airplane cabin. My face had been mashed to a pulp, and eating, an activity that uses nearly every muscle in the face, was extremely painful. My ankle that I had entered the fight with injured, had its natural healing process prolonged considerably. Financially, I had pocketed some money, mainly due to the fact that I had not had the time to spend it on a training camp. All in all, though, it was a near-total loss.

I learned I couldn't prove a faceless mob on the internet wrong, or make them eat their words. It was the people I knew, whispering in locker rooms and parking lots, that motivated me. In a strange way, all of their collective faces motivated me every day for the next year. I rehearsed over and over what I would text back to Ricardo's brother when the time came.

CHAPTER 22

I lay the large sheet of paper down on the kitchen table after clearing some odds and ends. It makes the satisfying sound of paper being unrolled, something I miss in the digital world. It's partially why I insisted the contractor give me a physical copy of the building plans. My father looks over my shoulder, tilting his head so that he can see through the lens of his glasses.

"What do you think?" I say. I brace myself a bit, not sure how he will react. His eyes run over the paper for a second before saying, "You're building a house?"

"Yes," I say, holding back a smile until he fully realizes what this is.

"But your house is beautiful, son." he says with a puzzled look.

"I'm gonna keep it."

His frugal alarm bells go off, and he leans away as if I just lit myself on fire. "You're building a *second* house?!"

"Dad, it's not just a second house. It's a guest house. And I wanna build it here, in your backyard."

He blinks and then points outside at his yard through the window. "You mean *here*?"

"Dad, you need help; you need me to look after you and Mom. I can live here, have my own space."

He places his hand on top of his head and rubs it slowly like he is massaging his brain to make room for this revelation.

"But it's—"

"The kids can come over whenever they want. Hell, they can live here."

"—so big . . ."

"It's a one-bedroom. It's like an apartment basically."

"The wife?"

I shift my weight uncomfortably, my only tell. Dad knows that we are divorced, but he still refers to her as my wife from time to time.

"She can stay at our house, no problem. It's better for us this way, Dad."

He stares out at the yard, probably envisioning what a small house planted in the center would look like. He breaks from his daydream and looks at me. "Son, how can you afford this?"

My father knows I have money, I have a nice house, I drive a nice truck. But I've never bought things just to have them. I've never been flashy with my money.

"Dad, it's fine. I have the money, trust me. I'm not going into the poorhouse for you, old-timer."

He looks down and I hear a crack in his voice, "Son, I . . ."

I finish his sentence. "I love you, Dad."

We have a little moment in the kitchen, and I mentally thank God for all the blessings he's given me. There was a time, not so long ago, when I would do crazy things to put food on the table. When I would have to leave my family in order to feed them.

It makes me think of China . . .

———•———

"Daddy, nooo!"

My daughter is having a tantrum on the floor, throwing herself down and crying uncontrollably. I tell myself that she's just tired and stressed. Everyone is.

Hurricane Sandy made landfall a week ago, hitting New Jersey particularly hard. Flooding, power outages, schools closed, businesses boarded up. My whole town looks like a war zone. And what am I doing? I'm training for a fight. Another UFC fight. The most important fight in my life. But just like before, life has dealt me a strange hand. I've spent the last week training in a dark gym with no power, using portable lights from any hardware store that isn't cleaned out. I'm also cutting weight, an awful experience under the best of circumstances. The cut from 205 pounds to 185 pounds cannot be accomplished by a few weeks of giving up chocolate and beer. I'm on week seven of 1800 calories a day. Even that has only gotten me to 207 pounds. In the next week, I will need to lose 20 more pounds, much of which will involve wringing every last ounce of water from my body in the final hours. I'm irritable, constantly hungry and cranky. My daughter's screaming isn't helpful.

As I think these thoughts, I feel a pang of guilt for making Isabelle's pain about me. As a fighter, you have to be selfish to an extent. Fighting isn't like any other job. It's a full-time job and an on-call job. When the call comes, you drop what you're doing and go in to work. I've seen fighters literally call off their weddings when the call came. I'm leaving my family in the middle of the worst storm in a century, flying to the other end of the planet to fight in China.

Isabelle doesn't understand this. I can never explain to her how fighting pays for her home, her clothes, her schooling. Even if she did understand, she would live in a car with me if it meant we could be together all the time. What's worse, she is growing up and beginning to understand. What her daddy does is dangerous; he can get hurt badly. She is not old enough to understand degrees of hurt, to distinguish minor and major injuries. Any hurt is scary to her, so she begs me not to go to the airport as she watches me pack my bags.

I channel my inner Ricardo and tell her that I have to go, as stoically as I can. I tell her that I need her to be strong and stop crying. In reality, I'm more pleading with her than telling her. I need her to tell me that she understands, to kiss me on the cheek and tell me that she loves me and will see me when I get back. But Isabelle can't do that, she's selfish like me. The difference is that kids are supposed to be selfish. Not fathers.

I leave the house, park at the airport, take the shuttle to the terminal. I'm in a haze the whole time, giving one-word grunts to attendants. I tell myself it's the weight cut, and maybe it is. But a part of me just feels like a piece of shit for leaving them.

I have a long, long flight to think about all this. To pass some time, I read the bible on an app on my phone. I don't do this as often as I should. I land on the story of Moses and the Pharaoh, and how the Pharaoh would harden his heart. Something about it struck me that I had to harden my heart as well. This is what it takes.

The idea gives me a bit of peace until I remember that the Pharaoh was the villain in the story.

CHAPTER 23

My Dad enters the truck, his daily dose of methadone giving him his typical contentedness. He might normally be impatient with me as I sit on my phone, texting. But right now, he simply sits next to me and waits. I scroll through my Instagram inbox, responding to one of the dozens or hundreds of messages I get every day from students around the world. I come across a comment that Gordon Ryan left on a post. It's typical Gordon stuff. The kid knows how to press buttons. I chuckle out loud at his latest antics. What I always marvel at with Gordon is how he has convinced the world that it's a persona. It's not. He is just about the same in real life as on social media.

"What's so funny?" asks my Dad

"Ah, just some of the shit Gordon says online is hilarious. The stones on this kid."

"That little shitkicker been brought down a peg yet?"

I put my phone away, "Nope. He just won ADCC like six months ago."

"He still gonna be something special?"

"Not *going* to be. He is. They're saying he's the best in the whole game right now."

My father chuckles and says, "Good for him. Must feel good. Didn't he start out with you?"

"Yup, me and Garry brought him up."

"And he was always like that, with the crown and all?"

He's referring to the literal crown that Gordon is famous for wearing at tournaments, something that only the best in the world could do and get away with. The second Gordon were to be submitted, or even edged out on points, he would have to eat that crown in humiliation. But it had never happened.

"Yeah, pretty much." I say. "But he earned that crown."

"There a story there?" Dad asks as we pull out of the parking lot.

"I got a hundred stories about that kid."

When you're young, the concept of aging, declining, not being as good as you are now, is so vague. Your first hint that it may actually happen to you is seeing it happen to those around you. I grew up training with Ricardo Almeida, Frankie Edgar, the Gracie family. But, one by one, I saw them all cede their status in some way. They never dropped off a cliff or became old men. It happens subtly. They are the lions of the gym. They don't get hurt, they don't take breaks, they don't have relationships or anything to distract them. Most of all, they don't have pressure. They are here to shock the world, to beat expectations.

But over time, your potential becomes thoroughly measured out. Media, fans, the internet; they all determine exactly how far they think you will go in your career. The worst part about this is that they often get it right. Then you go from the guy surprising everyone to the guy surprising no one. And all the while, a new guy is on your mats, running through everyone. All the attention is now on him. How far can he go? Where is the ceiling for him?

In the early 2010s, I'm still that guy. People still wonder about my ceiling. Can I win another ADCC trials? Can I make it in high-level MMA? I have a few surprises left, maybe more than a few. But in the meantime, I'm a teacher. And right now, I'm enjoying laying a beating on an arrogant prick of a purple belt.

He's fresh off another win at a local NAGA tournament. The kid wins everything. Gi or no gi, it doesn't matter. He was bad enough in the beginning as an arrogant white belt. But now, it's becoming apparent that he's actually very good. He not just big and strong, he's smart. He also works hard and shows up every day. The full package.

He walks into the gym with an extra swagger, like a king returning from another victory. He does everything but ask a teammate to wash his car. He even has a cute young girl on his arm, bringing her to witness the victory lap and run circles around some blue belts during practice. He's only been training for a few years at this point. He has a lot to learn. Technically, sure, but more as a man. In a weird way, I really like the kid. Despite all of our efforts to beat his attitude out of him when he was a white belt, he just wouldn't eat the humble pie. It's the sort of pathological confidence that you develop a respect for over time. You can beat the shit out of this kid, but you just can't beat the attitude out of him.

Then he starts getting really good. Now you *really* have a problem. Ego backed up with legitimate talent. While no one will say it to his face, everyone at Ocean County Jiu Jitsu knows that he's going to be special. And so does he.

So as I watch him high-fiving everyone, skipping warmups and generally parading himself around, I decide to give him a thorough ass-whooping. Maybe it's the voice of Ricardo Almeida in my mind. He would never let me prance around the gym like a peacock.

I pair up with him and begin the roll at a fast pace. At this moment in time, I am the superior grappler. I'm a dog who's been living on the streets; he's a dog who's been living inside. I throw him off with my physicality, forcing him to turtle, twist, roll, and shrimp his way back into defensible positions. All the while, I can't help but do a little shit-talking in his ear. Nothing too bad, although I can't stop myself from winking at his girlfriend once or twice while Gordon is flattened out beneath me. She grins and giggles softly, pulling her hair in front of her mouth.

And yet, I also feel the kid getting his composure back as the minutes tick on. He starts to right the ship, scoring a few minor victories like getting his frames in by shifting his weight to the side. I bait him with a faux submission attempt, one that I used last month on him.

This time, he ignores the trap. As his breathing gets under control, the veil that is constantly over him is briefly lifted. I see his face, bright red with sweat and frustration. I see a kid that needs to win, a kid that doesn't acknowledge losing like a normal person. I could beat him like this every day; it wouldn't matter. He would just keep coming back for more.

When we finish out the roll, I am surprisingly tired. A year from now, he'll be as good as Garry. Five years from now . . . I'd better get my licks in while I can. Who knows what his ceiling is.

"You know I own your ass, right?" I ask him.

He blinks rapidly and heaves out between big breaths, "If you need to take a break I can give you a minute."

I laugh from incredulity. The stones on this kid. I love it.

CHAPTER 24

"Oh, you okay man?"

My partner is dropped on one knee. He bites down on his mouthpiece hard and hisses out a long breath. He stands up and nods rapidly.

"You okay?" I say again, unconvinced.

He mumbles in the affirmative and attempts to put his hands up to resume. As his hands go up, they immediately drop and he takes a step back. He bobs up and down a time or two. He took a hard shot at the end of a nearly two-hour training session and five or so minutes of sparring with me. At Ricardo Almeida's, we don't wear headgear. We use sixteen-ounce gloves to dull the impacts. But the tradeoff is that we spar with the full intensity of an MMA fight. Getting hit is part of the game, so we hit each other. I'm a heavy hitter. No one looks forward to sparring with me.

I give him a second to get his bearings, and we resume. He circles, feels out his range, but he's changed. He is staying busy, but I can tell he doesn't really have his legs under him yet. It's just a display to run out the final minutes on the clock. I'm okay with this; there's no need to kill people in the gym. There will be another round tomorrow night, then the next night. I play along, feigning some jabs and level changes.

As the seconds tick down, he's feeling confident again. He charges forward, swinging his hands, but he's still not moving quite right. At the exact moment the buzzer rings to mark the end of the round, I clip him coming in with my right hand. I see his face go dead from the impact. His eyes roll back and his hands drop. I have a brief second of horror as I watch him fall limp to the ground. His head smacks the mat, and the impact jolts him awake. This happens occasionally, where a person is knocked out for a mere second and the impact of their head on the mats jolts them back to life. It happens so fast, I am the only one to notice.

He slowly returns to his feet, I kneel and help him up. The action has stopped across the gym as fighters gather themselves before the next round. Most of them notice my training partner slow to get up. Reactions range from some shouts and hollers to some questions of concern. The truth is, knockouts like this are common. Rarely is anyone knocked out cold, but people get "clipped" every day.

I help him up and ask the obligatory "Are you okay?"

He says the only answer that's acceptable: that he's fine. I take a moment to look into his glassy eyes. He is squinting at the window to the academy and the bright lights coming from outside. More than that, his face is contorted in actual pain.

A timer buzzes. Ricardo calls the start of another round. I put my hand on my partner's shoulder. "You can take a round off."

Maybe I didn't say it the right way, but he looks at me like the diseased gazelle, being cleaved by the herd. He wouldn't take a round off if he was bleeding out.

"No, I'm good, I'm good." He hits himself in the head twice to signify as much. He wanders away to find his next partner.

Just another night.

CHAPTER 25

"I thought you said you were done fighting, after you knocked out that one guy."

We drive through the streets with unusual smoothness. There are few commuters on the streets these days. Not since the lockdowns. Some people are out, the blue-collar folks that America needs to work for everything to keep happening. Warehouse workers, drivers, and people like me: gym owners. I still think of myself as just another lunch-box guy sometimes. After all, I break my back day after day at the gym. I come home just as tired as the construction worker. The only difference is the house I come home to.

But I have problems that a bricklayer doesn't have. I'm currently being sued by some asshole. I have thirty academies, and at least one of them has some bullshit going on at any given time that I need to get involved in. And of course, I recently was thrown into a game of financial chicken with the government, who has tried to shut my academy down during the pandemic. I have multiple streams of income, and I pride myself in not needing any single one. But I never really considered that *all* of them could be put in jeopardy at once.

"Hey! You punch drunk on me?"

"Sorry." I mumble. "Jason Lambert."

"Jesus Christ, I knew it. No, you're Tom, Tom DeBlass."

"No, I mean that's the guy I knocked out. His name was Jas—"

I stop as I catch the slight smile appearing at the corners of my Dad's mouth. I nod as an acknowledgement that he got me on that one. Then I start over, "Yeah, well, I guess I never say never."

"What was it about Jason that made you want to stop?"

I go back in my mind to seeing the glassy look in Jason's eyes. A look I'll never, ever forget.

"That's it, Tom! Finish him!"

I hear the words of my corner, but I just can't cover the distance in time before Jason is back up to his feet. He gets his hands up and seems to move intelligently, but with a major tell: he wobbles a bit when he puts his weight on his back foot.

It's a motion most people in the crowd won't notice. You have to be close, and you have to know what to look for. Even the referee notices, with his trained eye that has probably seen a hundred knockouts. I know what I have to do.

You have to be ruthless in fighting, so I press my advantage. I stalk him around the cage, not charging him but constantly shrinking the box he is in. Occasionally, he will lash out with some lunging strikes. Each time he does, I take the opportunity to land my own. His glancing blows are dangerous, but sloppy. Mine are precise and heavy. I balance between pressing him and rushing. Plenty of time left in this three-round fight.

Finally, I land the blow I've been waiting for, not ten seconds after the last one. It's a solid power punch that lands right on his jaw. I feel no resistance as I land it, just his jaw snapping his head around. I feel a flick of his sweat land on my arm. Jason drops to the ground. He's not out, and maybe he can keep fighting. But the referee has seen enough. Dropped twice within a short period of time is enough for him to call it. He dives forward, waving his hands to signal that the fight is over.

My corner storms the ring. Thousands of fans in the Taj Mahal celebrate. The coveted knockout, the ultimate fan service. It should be one of the happiest moments of my life. I get to go home uninjured, with a win bonus and a two-fight winning streak. The next fight will be bigger, more money. My team will celebrate with me tonight. I won't go to the hospital.

I stare at Jason. Red-faced, bleeding, he protests the stoppage, but I can see in his eyes that he's still glassy. He *will* go to a hospital. They'll fix him up as best they can. But the real damage can't be fixed with stitches or surgery. In fact, it can hardly be detected at all. Jason has had a long career. I'm just the latest in a long line of people to knock him out in the cage, never mind sparring sessions.

I don't scream at the sky or jump onto the cage. I don't look into the camera or try and find Scott Coker in the crowd. I take a knee beside Jason and lean in close.

The referee momentarily grabs me, worried that I'm not aware the fight is over and am surging in for more punishment. I yell over the crowd noise to Jason, telling him that he is going to be fine and thanking him for the fight. He's out of it, doesn't really acknowledge me. I must have some sort of concerned look on my face, because the referee shoos me off and assures me that Jason is all right before patting me on the back.

Is he all right? I suppose it depends how you define it. He'll survive, of course, if you want to set the bar that low. But this is a man who just got a little bit more brain damage on his scorecard. A man who, I had found out earlier, has a daughter. I think of my daughter, whose cries get louder and more forceful every time I leave to fight. She begs me not to go, she doesn't want me to get hurt. Tonight I'm going to come home healthy, but at what price? I sent another man home to his daughter with brain damage. I try to think of him as my enemy and the fight as just work. But it's hard. His name is Jason. And he has a family.

I celebrate in the cage, I celebrate all night. But the thought lingers in the back of my head. You'll never be able to win without hurting people. You'll never be able to lose without getting hurt. It doesn't feel right to me, and I realize no victory will ever feel right again.

"So you decided to stop then?"

"Yeah, that was my last MMA fight. I was scheduled for one more, and it would have been a big one."

"That was the King Mo guy?" my father says. He remembers when I told him about the fight, which would have been no doubt the biggest fight of my career. I was forced to pull out twice due to injuries. Unknown to me, King Mo was having his own health issues as well during this time. Serious ones. Could I have beaten him? Absolutely, but it wouldn't have been a gimme by any stretch.

Winning would have catapulted me into the top five names in the Bellator. I would have surely been matched up with guys like Phil Davis or Quinton "Rampage" Jackson next.

"Yeah, but that fight got called off twice. Can't believe my luck."

"Maybe it wasn't luck at all," Dad says while gazing out the car window.

I know what he's getting at. "Yeah, you're probably right. Would have been good for my wallet but not my body."

"Might not have been good for your soul, either."

It's an unusually deep observation from my father, who knows a thing or two about matters of the soul. I don't reply to him, because he's right and there's not much to say. It's far more rewarding to be a Brazilian jiu-jitsu instructor, although back in 2014 at the peak of my MMA career, the Tom DeBlass Association didn't even exist yet. I was still grinding out classes and MMA training, driving halfway across New Jersey and New York every week. But things were about to change for me. About a year after I left MMA, jiu-jitsu wouldn't just be paying the bills anymore.

CHAPTER 26

I don't get to train with Gordon as much as I used to. He's under my first black belt, Garry Tonon, nowadays. When I do train with him, it's a pleasure to see him growing by leaps and bounds.

But in other ways, it sucks.

Today, Gordon seems to have a single-minded focus on my legs. He scoots towards me, under me, and fights to get his legs to the inside position. I am no stranger to leg attacks, but even my brain is having trouble staying one step ahead. Gordon weaves his legs into mine, changing the puzzle frequently. As I move to escape, he smoothly reconfigures his attacks. I find myself relying more on my instincts to know when I am in danger, but the path to safety isn't clear. Gordon gets a tap from me, then another a few minutes later. I watch his eyes, watch his body. He is more cerebral than I remember him.

We finish the round and I slap him on the back and smile.

"You're getting good at that stuff," I say while pointing to his legs.

"Yeah, it's something we're been working on all the time." Gordon and Garry have been spending a lot of time at Renzo's, especially with a guy named Eddie Cummings. An up-and-comer in the game, Eddie and his coach, John Danaher, had been working together with a few guys on the downstairs mat. Not quite a class, just sort of an open mat, without the open part.

"He likes the leg stuff, huh?" I say.

Gary shakes his head, "No, it's more than that. It's everything."

"Oh yeah? Like what?"

"I dunno, he just has, like, a system. I've never seen anything like it."

"A system for leg locks?"

"Leg locks are a part of it, sure. But it's a system for the whole game, like big-picture stuff. It's not even really techniques. It's like the way he thinks. There's always a plan."

"Are you talking about Eddie or John?"

"Both."

I take a moment to appreciate the situation. Gordon and Garry have become something special, and also something out of my control. Not just my students anymore, they are a product of the many students and teachers they've sought out, and they're better for it. I see myself in their games, but I also see others. I've taught Gordon a lot, but maybe it's time he teaches me something.

I scoot towards him and start recreating a position. "Show me what you did from here . . ."

CHAPTER 27

I sit in my office at Ocean County Jiu-Jitsu. Well, these days, it's more like *the* office because it belongs more to Craig and Danielle than it does me. Despite the fact that I own it and pay for it, I am spending less time here than ever.

I've always been a mat rat and a competitor. I've never particularly gotten off on processing invoices, thinking about marketing, or making spreadsheets. I was unaware how much that was costing me until the pandemic hit us. I'm embarrassed to say that I had gotten so busy, I rarely had time to look closely at the checks that came through every month from Ocean County BJJ or any of the other schools in the association. But the lockdowns made all school owners look closely at their books. A couple things became painfully clear.

Many students called and cancelled their memberships or put them on hold. But some of them, it turns out, weren't paying in the first place because of credit cards that had been declined or expired. Other students had dropped off the radar, probably planning to return but maybe not knowing that we had even reopened.

And then there was the little things. Corners I hadn't cleaned out in awhile. Cabinets not organized, windows that needed some Windex. Running the most successful academy in New Jersey comes down to a simple formula: You have the cleanest, best-looking, friendliest, most flexible academy with the best instructors, the best students, and the best culture. In the entire state. It's not easy, but it is simple.

Although the Tom DeBlass name surely brought many students through the door, the truth was that coasting on that name recognition would give the hundred other gyms in the area the opening they needed. Gyms with young, hungry instructors would take my lunch money if they could. Not because anyone hates anyone. But we're competitors, and they need to eat too.

It's in this landscape that I made one of the best decisions I've ever made. I hired two people to run the operations of the academy. The first was my black belt Craig Izzo. They second was a student, Danielle, who had been training with us for awhile.

As I sit in the office and review the profit-and-loss statement from this quarter, I look at them twice and then three times in disbelief. In the worst business climate in a decade, we have somehow achieved record enrollment. I grab a pen nearby to write a note to the team of congratulations. I notice for the first time that the office is unusually organized. Boxes on the floor have been stacked and labeled in a corner. Gis are hanging up, Post-it notes are arranged neatly in a column. Each note has names and numbers on them, a list of prospects or lapsed students that Danielle will be personally calling tonight. She'll ask after their health and if there is anything we can do to get them back in the gym. This is something I always struggled with finding time for. But now, anyone who drops off gets a call, and a surprising number of them return when they are invited back.

I look out to the main floor of the gym where Craig is talking to a visitor. Under his leadership, everyone who walks into Ocean County BJJ gets the same treatment. We've developed a script, refined it, and taught it to the instructors. The rest of the students aren't taught it, but they see their teachers being friendly and helpful to new arrivals, and they do the same. They don't follow a script, but they follow the culture.

All of this allows me to focus on teaching and training. I still set the direction of the academy, but I trust the team to carry it out in the way they know works best. Why the hell didn't I do this sooner? I look at my clock. Time to get back; I'm talking to the builder this afternoon for the new condo in my parents' backyard. As I rise, I feel an ache in my back and other parts of my body. I think I'm getting sick or maybe even some nagging back pain from my old ADCC injury.

As I make to leave, I spot a Post-it note from Danielle for me. It reads:

ONE FC *guy emailed again, they need contract?*

***

"You okay?"

Garry approaches me in the warm-up pen, where a dozen competitors are stretching, doing jumping jacks, rolling light, or even rolling hard. Garry is working as a coach for me today, and he's already an accomplished enough competitor that, as he navigates the pen, a few eyes follow him curiously. But Garry isn't fighting. He's supporting me in my grappling superfight against Nelson Puentes. He's lugging around my bag and other odds and ends. Part of a coach's job is sometimes to be a pack mule for their competitors.

He notices something, even if he can't put his finger on it. One minute I'm bouncing around trying to work up a sweat and get loose. The next, I'm pacing sluggishly with my arms at my hips and a look of frustration.

"Yeah, I'm fine," I say, pursing my lower lip and nodding my head dismissively. My opponent, and his teammates, are likely within earshot of me. I beckon Garry closer to where no one can overhear us.

"I think I tweaked my back." I say it as casually as I can.

Garry's face is blank for a second while he processes. Then he says cautiously, "Okay, so what are we talking here?"

I bob my head back and forth, then smile and chuckle for no reason. Garry has a look of confusion, then understanding crosses over his eyes. It's probably not prudent for me to be pointing at my back or letting Garry put his hand on the spot where it hurts. Not with so many people around. Truth be told, I don't even know what my opponent really looks like, or what he's wearing.

"We're talking I can barely walk, that's what were fucking talking about." I say in an oddly casual tone.

Garry doesn't say anything, he just lets me walk around a bit and figure out my various ranges of motions. It's not good. A few minutes ago I took a big vertical leap and, upon landing, felt like a hitman had walked up behind me and stuck a knife in my back. Within seconds, my posture had been reduced to something like a homeless man limping around. I finally settled on just standing still and pretending to breathe hard, so maybe people would think that I was warmed up and ready to go.

I lie down on the mat in a guard-like position, move around a bit, and tell Gary to do some light rolling with me. It doesn't feel good, but it also won't kill me. I go to stand up, and another explosion of pain hits my body as my spine straightens. I tell Gary that there's a new plan. The old plan was to go wherever the fight went. The new plan is to hope it goes to the mat and stays there. I see an official walking towards me, looking at me and then down at his clipboard.

"Tom, we're going to have you over here on Mat One."

Garry is spouting off a list of instructions of "if he does this, then do that." I halt him with a slap on the back and a small grin. It's time to fight.

CHAPTER 28

The mats are cleared; the announcer calls everyone's attention to the center mats. BJJ is changing. Superfights are common in every tournament now. Whereas a handful of men used to dominate grappling year after year, now there are more hot prospects than I can keep up with.

Case in point: I know next to nothing about my superfight opponent, Nelson Padilla. I take one look at the silly upside-down panda on his bright colored rash guard and make a guess that he's a new school guy.

My back is dormant for a few seconds, then a slight movement results in a sharp pain. Then it goes off as if someone simply flipped a switch. It reiterates the urgency of getting this fight down to the mats as quickly as possible. At the same time, it's not so urgent that I will pull guard or allow a takedown.

The ref dramatically cuts the air with his arm, and Nelson approaches me immediately and begins the opening moves. Jiu-jitsu standing up is each man feeling out range, timing, reflexes, and then putting it all together in that one perfect moment. I recognize Nelson doing that to me. In ten seconds, we fight about a dozen invisible battles for inside position, head position, control of the neck, testing the balance. I have the skill and power, my back notwithstanding, to keep him occupied for awhile on the feet. But right now, every second spent standing is a second where I can't win. Or, worse, a second where he can realize I am injured.

I don't tip him off as much as I communicate with my body that I'm not going to be the one to pull the trigger, and that he might as well go ahead. I don't know whether he picks up on this or was intent on doing what he did anyways. He sits down abruptly, practically underneath me, and lifts my 200-pound body into the air for a beautiful entry to a leg entanglement. In the scramble, he misses the position he wants narrowly and settles into a neutral position. He smoothly transitions to an inside heelhook, then an outside one, then a kneebar. It's a tangle of legs and limbs to most people, but to me and him it's a flowchart of connected positions.

I have Garry and Gordon to thank in the moment. Suddenly their months of exploiting my lack of leglock defenses are paying dividends. I know every position now, when to turn the heel in, when to spin out, and when to cross my legs. And in case I forget, I have the practiced voice of Garry a few feet away.

Gary is far from the ADD maniac I met years ago. He speaks to me with the commanding voice of any good coach. He doesn't scream, he calmly walks me through my path of every position. Nelson, for the briefest of moments, glances at my eyes, and I see frustration. Garry is practically reading his mind, calling out Nelson's options seconds before he does them.

Nelson has opportunities to return the match to standing, but he doesn't take them. He wants to fight for legs, not realizing that I can barely stand. After his initial flurry of attacks, I gradually begin to turn the tide. I begin collecting legs of my own, chaining attacks. What begins as both of us jockeying for position becomes him putting out fires as I threaten knees, heels, and ankles. Finally, I scoop my forearm deep on his heel and twist my spine and hips. He taps.

There's applause, some rowdy cheering from Garry and the guys. I never scream or run around after matches. Which is good, because if I had done that in this moment, I may have been carted out of there on a stretcher.

I went to stand up, and my back exploded in pain like there was an invisible ceiling five feet off of ground. I slouched over like an old man.

"No offense, of course." I say to my father in a moment of self-consciousness.

"I *am* an old man, so you're forgiven. What happened then?"

"The referee raised my hand, I shook hands with Nelson. No one seemed to notice I could barely walk. Garry met me off the mats and congratulated me, but he knew what I knew: I had fucked up my back just a week before the ADCC trials."

CHAPTER 29

It came on gradually, just another bug. A mild fever, maybe a gross cough to go with it. I'm a fighter; I've hobbled into the UFC octagon. My job is to show up and teach classes. As long as there's one student that is willing to learn, I am teaching. When you own a gym, you say goodbye to vacation for a long time. You say goodbye to free time at night, to company healthcare and a 401k. Your back is bothering you? Too bad, class is in an hour. This was my mentality, and it's made me successful. Shrugging off a little bug was easy to do.

Then came the chest pains—again, gradually. It started as just a odd bubbling sensation inside my chest when I took a deep breath. A few days later I could feel it when I took even a normal breath. By then, I was breathing out of my mouth without even noticing it. Sparring in class became difficult, and suddenly I couldn't do it at all.

One night, I lay on my back to try and get the breathing under control. I found I could not take a deep breath; I could only take small sips of air. I tried to inhale deeply, once, twice, and three times. Each time I was unsuccessful, I would feel and even hear the oozing sound of air pushing through my chest. What began as more of an experiment became a major physical problem. I lay on the ground and felt my breathing spiral out of control. I began to make a wheezing sound, which threw me even more out of control. My chest was rising and falling a few inches now, like it had a mind of its own. I tried to slow down my breathing but I was along for the ride now. I thought maybe it was a panic attack, or maybe even a heart attack.

This continued for nearly an hour. During that time, I had nothing to do but stare at the ceiling and consider my life and death. I vacillated between peace and despair. I wondered who would find me and prayed it wouldn't be my daughter or son. I prayed to God to take me, then I prayed for him to leave me here long enough to take care of my Mother and Father and the kids.

Eventually I go to sleep, able to breathe but with a steady gurgling sound. I wake up before dawn, now only able to take the most shallow of breaths. I lumber out to the family room, and as I do, I feel dizzy. My mother looks at me, surprised that I'm awake this early. Her expression goes from surprise to concern in a second. I take another step, then black out. I am awake what seems like a short time later. My mother is talking to me, relatively calmly. She sets me up on the couch and starts asking questions. She works at a hospital and knows how to check for symptoms. I don't tell her about last night, not how serious it was anyways.

I get some energy back and even eat some food. I tell her to get off to work, I'm just feeling a little lightheaded. I cough a little, first lightly and then full-on rasps that have me bending over. My throat feels like it's filled with peanut butter, a thought that seems funny for a second before I hit the floor and vomit a steady stream of blood and pus for what might have been a full second or two.

My first thought is that I'm ruining her nice living room, which looks like the set of a horror film now. She begins giving me loud, firm instructions. The rest is a blur, but we somehow get in her car and to a hospital.

It's a sudden and abrupt turning of the page in my life, which would never be the same after that day. I woke up in an empty room, connected to what seemed like a hundred machines. It felt like if I moved at all, each one would break and I would die. I looked around with only my eyes, trying to get a sense of where I was. I don't know how much time went by, but it felt like an hour, during which time I made wild stories about what had happened and why I was here. One thing I was able to rule out early was that I had COVID. I had already gotten it in November around the time I last competed. I remember reading somewhere that you couldn't get it twice, or not for a long time.

As these thoughts swirled around my head, a person came in the room. They were covered from head to toe in a hazmat suit of some sort. I couldn't see anything about them other than they were human. It approached me and spoke in a muffled voice that I had to strain to hear. It was a woman, a nurse. She didn't talk to me as much as she delivered a report with everything I needed to know.

I had been in the hospital for more than a day. I was very sick with pneumonia. I'd had COVID as recently as last week and still did but was past symptoms. She rattled off a number of medications that were now in my body, and more would be coming every hour. A large portion of these would be steroids to help power my lungs and heart. I'm not a doctor and I wasn't in the best position to take notes, but this is what I remember.

I argued in vain that I'd already had COVID months ago. I couldn't get it twice, right? She explained that it was rare but very possible. New Jersey had some sort of new variant that could infect people as if they had never had it to begin with.

I've been in a lot of hospitals. One thing I've learned is that doctors and nurses will never tell you you're going to die unless they are one hundred percent certain. They also don't make predictions or use percentages. Still, it was worth a shot. I asked the nurse if I was likely to live. She said something that chilled my blood:

"You're very sick Thomas."

That sounded like a no to me, and it sure as hell wasn't a yes.

I asked if I could see my family, even though the answer was obvious by her attire. No family, no phone, nothing. I needed to rest, and if I wanted to entertain myself, then I could lie here and think about my life. So I did.

I imagined that it was just a few weeks ago, and I was driving my Dad to the clinic again. Maybe we're still talking about the story, maybe we're talking about the kids. Anything would be a blessing. I promise myself that when I see him again, we will finish the story. Then we'll talk about him. I want to hear about his life next. All of it. It's what I should have done from the start. Something about this little promise gives me some hope, and I drift back to sleep. I dream strange dreams of the past.

•—•—•

It was a strange time for me in 2014, stuck in between two worlds. In the world of MMA, I was in resurgence. Two Bellator fights, two wins. I had become a ranked fighter, and Bellator had decided to put me in play. Managers were talking; I was getting text messages every hour about the latest curveballs in contract negotiations. Muhammed Lawal, a.k.a. King Mo, was looking increasingly likely to be my next opponent.

But other things were happening in the world of jiu-jitsu. No longer the dinky little sport in high school gyms, jiu-jitsu was starting to be a viable career choice. Not just as a school owner, which had always been possible. But as a competitor. Sponsorships, instructionals, and even respectable fight purses were now possible.

I was still young, strong, and talented. I wanted it all. MMA belts, and BJJ medals around my neck. A part of me thought I could do it. I could win it all through sheer grit and stubbornness. I could grind out any pain, any opponent, I could grind out my life.

But another part of me knew that I was not going to be able to sustain it all. In both sports, there were a hundred other guys that wanted the same thing I did. All of them were tough, all of them were talented, and most of them were focusing on one sport at a time.

On paper, it wasn't a hard decision. Professional MMA leaves ninety-nine percent of its athletes broke and broken at their career's end. Professional grappling does not. Beyond that, there was a purity to grappling that I enjoyed. You register for the tournament, you get your bracket, you compete. No callouts on the mic, no psychological warfare with a promoter, no stall negotiations and last-minute opponent changes.You can fight three times a year in an MMA promotion, or compete a dozen times a year and run your own school.

In my head, the decision wasn't as easy. Competition is a strange addiction. They say drug addicts begin by chasing the high but eventually they are simply trying to avoid the low of coming off. By the end, the high doesn't feel quite as good as it used to, and the low feels worse than ever before. For a psychotic competitor, the wins are the high, and the losses are the low. The high fades too fast; the low lasts longer each time. The awareness sets in that each win will be harder to get as your competition gets tougher and your body gets older. It's a losing equation for normal people. But that's why we call ourselves *psychotic* competitors. It's never enough for us. The title doesn't matter as much as the feeling of winning, or maybe the relief of not losing.

So the smart play was leaving MMA and going back to grappling and teaching full time. But I just couldn't close the door on fighting. When the King Mo fight fell through, I knew that was probably it. Probably.

I went into ADCC trials more seriously injured than I was willing to admit to myself. But sometimes it's okay to embrace your inner meathead. The day of the tournament, I took a shot of Toradol, a nonsteroidal painkiller. It's essentially what they give people before surgeries. It's perfectly possible to turn off the part of your brain that thinks about long-term repercussions of competing with a bulged disc. It helps to have guys, other psychotic competitors, with you as well.

My semi final match was against Shohin Ghaffari. Everyone was good, really good, at this level. Shohin was an expert at leg attacks and heelhooks, ahead of the game in some ways. ADCC 2014 was still a clash of the old and the new. Some fighters were still working their closed guards and pressure passes, while others weren't passing guard at all and relentlessly attacking anything from the knee down..

Shinho and I fought an intense match. I worked my aggressive top game, running him down like a dog and closing every inch of space. There was a rhythm to the match, several seconds of posturing and preparation followed by an explosion from one of us. In ADCC, there is too much at stake. I think I even grabbed his throat with my hand at one point. It's hard to conceive of, but at the close of the match the score was exactly 0–0. My back was holding up, mainly due to the Toradol. Somewhere in the back of my mind I knew that nothing was free. The body would collect its toll eventually, when the numbing effect wore off.

The bell rang, saving me from a tough spot in the turtle position. Before we could even stand, the official barked out, "Three minutes overtime, points immediately, get up please!"

He physically pulled me up and to the center of the mat. I knew the rules of ADCC, but after ten minutes of fighting your higher brain largely switches off. All I really understood was that I had to keep going.

Garry was in the corner, leaning forward in his chair intently. The little ADD kid that walked into my gym years ago was gone. Garry was now speaking to me in the calm, articulated words of a coach. He didn't scream, he didn't say generic encouragement. He was the higher brain that I needed.

When points are enabled in BJJ, especially in overtime, matches tend to play out like an old Western movie. Each gunslinger hovers his hand over his six-shooter, waiting for the right moment to draw. One shot could be all it takes. Shinho and I locked up in a standing clinch and battled for posture, inside position, and head control. Although it may have looked like two meatheads in a stalemate, it was the tactical battle for the best possible moment to unleash your opening salvo. I finally had the perfect combination of all these things to explode underneath him and latch onto his leg. I ran him to the ground like a starving animal with thirty seconds left. It was enough to secure the decision and advance me to the finals.

I was given some time between matches to rest, rehydrate, change shirts, and, most importantly, tend to any injuries. I had none, at least not that I could feel. My back still felt numb, but it was gradually giving way to tingling and other sensations as the day went on. Nothing hurt, but there was a strange ache that was making itself known.

I stuffed the feeling down. I would deal with it later. The next match was all that mattered. Even as I thought this, my mind was already thinking ahead. *What about the championships? How will you even train?*

I didn't know, it didn't matter. I hadn't come this far by worrying about the future. All I had to worry about was James Friedrich. He was an up-and-comer from Atos, a Southern California academy (by now, several) founded and ran by Andre Galvao.

I had fought Andre Galvao once, in the first round of the ADCC absolute division in the championships. He had beat me soundly, and I respected him. I didn't give much thought to the fact that I was fighting one of his students, but I'd be lying if I said I didn't give *any* thought to it.

He immediately sat to guard, a bold move that actually costs you points in the ADCC ruleset. The ADCC organizers designed the rules to encourage aggressive play with takedowns. It was a choice that gave me a lot of information right away. He was a bottom player, enough that he was willing to put himself behind right away to play his game.

Which was fine. I was a Ricardo Almeida black belt. We are not known for playing mind games or four-dimensional chess on the mats. I dove right into his guard.

Every match has a different story, a different feel. My previous match had been a contest of strength and energy: two titans, clashing against one another. But in the finals, a chess match emerged. James was clearly a leglock specialist, and thanks to Garry and Gordon I was a sort of defensive specialist. What followed was ten minutes of careful, tactical positioning in a variety of leg entanglements. While James's corner was largely silent, Garry methodically talked me through everything.

At a critical moment, James got me into a tough position where he came close to getting his signature heelhook. I managed to turn it around and get on top, scoring the first points of the match. James desperately worked from the bottom to get ahold of my leg again, but I pressed my advantage and stayed on top. With just seconds left, James managed to finally roll onto my leg and wrench it with everything he had, I took one of the few options available: I gave him my back to escape. James dove onto my back with all the urgency of a losing fighter. The chess match was over; it was a brawl from here on out. He got his first hook in, needing only one more to score his own points, which would be enough to end my hopes of being a two-time ADCC trials winner.

Garry's voice reached a new level of intensity, screaming that I was not to let his second hook in. James's normally smooth movements had given way to kicking, grunting, and panting. The crowd in the gym was animated, some attempting to coach and others simply shouting incoherently. It had all the intensity of two men fighting for their lives. This was everything for us. Irrational as it was, in our minds there was nothing worth winning outside of this single match.

I fended off James's second leg with my free arm, reaching blindly behind my back to feel for it and ward it off. James's face was inches from mine. I could feel the heat from his breath, his desperate gasps in those last seconds, but he didn't get it his leg in place. I felt the referee touch his hands to our backs, signaling that the match was over.

I leapt up and screamed like a mad Viking. The wave of euphoria hit my body. James turned away and covered his face with his hands. At this level, no one is happy to simply do well. You come to win, and there can only be one winner. Everyone else is a loser.

That night, after the parties, the back slaps, and the photos, I come home, take a shower, and see the gold medal in my bag. Very few people have won ADCC trials twice, or consecutively. I'm one of the best grapplers in the world. I live in a big house, my kids are happy, my family loves me. But I don't think about that. I can only think about the next one.

I put the medal in a drawer and set my alarm for five in the morning. Another full day of training tomorrow. As I lie down, I begin to breathe more laboriously. My breath quickens and deepens, but each time I get a little less air. I feel myself sinking into my bed, and I call for help.

I hear footsteps rushing into the room, and my father is there, moving faster than he has any right to. His strong arms clasp my hands. I can see the edges of the bed forming like a coffin made of bedsheets. More hands grasp me and try to pull me up. My mother is in the room. Everyone is talking over each other, barking orders, saying my name. I continue to wheeze, but I'm disappearing beneath the sheets now, my view of my mother and father disappearing. I feel smaller hands grab my arms now, and I hear the muffled cries of Thomas and Isabelle using all their strength to join the effort to pull me back.

I fall through the bed and into a bright, cold room. The hands are still there, but they are also cold and rubbery. The muffled voices are far away, then get closer and change. The sounds of machinery and alarms also emerge from the whiteness and get closer—or louder; I can't tell.

My vision goes from blurry to clear very slowly. The white light makes me briefly wonder if I am in heaven. But other sensory information begins to emerge. Heaven, I assume, doesn't have a particular smell. If it does, it doesn't smell like this: the stark, sterile smell . . . of a hospital.

People are crowded around me. Tubes are running into me. Everyone is talking, but no one is talking to me. I feel too weak to move or even talk. In fact, I literally feel too weak to move my eyes around. The figures are all wearing full body suits. I cannot see any faces, and their voices come out as muffled jargon that I doubt I would understand anyways. I may not understand their words, but I do understand their tone. It's not unlike the voice of a coach yelling at his student from behind a barrier during a BJJ match. It has that urgency, that intensity.

I feel real fear now, because I don't hear doctors and nurses talk like this unless the situation is dire. I think back to restraining my Dad in a hospital more than a decade ago. The chaos in the room that evening, I feel it now.

Am I about to die?

CHAPTER 30

The doctor walks in and begins speaking immediately. No doubt overwhelmed by patients and hardened by the past year, he speaks to me without emotion, without delicacy. It's an almost refreshing change of treatment from my normal life, where my students treat me with the highest respect.

"Well, you had a really rough go there for about four days, but I think you're going to pull through, no thanks to you."

I frown and say, "What do you mean?" I am struck by the voice that speaks the words. It's the voice of an old man that smokes a carton of cigarettes a day. There's no way it could be mine, and yet I only hear it when my lips move. I sound like shit.

He doesn't parse his words, "Whatever you're doing to yourself, it's going to kill you."

"Yeah," I say, "I know. I've been doing martial arts all my life, and you gotta understand, I've . . ."

I think better of telling him my woes. In all likelihood, he has seen people die around the clock for the past month. I could tell him about every medal, every submission, every knockout. None of it would impress him. He merely looks at me forensically, with the detached discipline of a medical doctor.

He puts his hand up to indicate he's heard enough, "You're not hearing me. You will be dead if you continue to push yourself like this. Your children will bury you. You need light to moderate exercise, nothing more. It's important that you rest and sleep more. No sleeping medication or relaxers. As of today, whatever your shelf life is as an athlete, I'm telling you that it's expired. It's time to stop."

He said it with a finality that made it feel like he had scored a walk-off knockout. He wasn't going to argue with me. In fact, he didn't even expect me to listen to him. The fact that he had no attachment of interest in me whatsoever told me that he was right. No one had ever spoken to me quite like this, and I didn't know what to say. He breezed through my chart, told me what my upcoming discharge would look like. What I could and could not do for the next few days. Bottom line, I would be out tomorrow.

"Can my family come and see me?"

Again, he didn't look up, "No, the quarantine rules will apply for sometime; I'm sorry about that. But the nurse brought your phone, and you can use it to video chat with them."

"My father, he wasn't feeling good," I start to say. The doctor anticipates my next question.

"Your father is here."

"Someone should tell him to go home if I can't have visitors."

He stops, then looks up from his chart. For the first time I see that he is exhausted, lines streaking his face through his mask and face shield.

"No, he's hospitalized here."

I stutter and am quiet for a second as my mind processes what I just heard.

"He's—"

"He's not well, Mr. DeBlass. He's in intensive care, but he's very ill."

"Do you think . . ."

Again the doctor is stoic. "He's very ill."

We sit in silence as I blink a few times.

———◆———

I speak with my mother and kids on FaceTime. I am careful to wait until I look more or less like the father that they remember. A few days ago they may not have even recognized me. My voice is still scratchy, and my beard and hair are too long but other than that I look okay. I do *not* feel okay, though. I am still too weak to even take a brisk walk around the hospital. I still feel a wheezing sound in my chest, bubbling up with every deep inhale.

My kids have odd questions. Did I sleep too much? Am I sneezing? Can I still drop them off at school? Can I come to the kitchen in an hour? They really do not have a concept of hospitalization. They speak to me like this often, because I travel often. In that sense, I might as well be gone at another seminar for them. Isabelle gets it more and more, though, and I see some looks of real concern on her face. The two men in her life are in a hospital, very suddenly. She couldn't talk to either of us for days. It motivates me to get the hell out of here.

My mother ushers the kids off to where their mother is waiting for them, off-screen. Delilah, despite our separation, is one hundred percent in the game as a parent and as simply a person with empathy. She loves my father; they've always gotten along.

When my children are safely out of earshot, my mother and I talk about my father. We exchange information rapidly, each filling out pieces of the puzzle about when it happened, how it happened, and what we know. We avoid offering any sort of prognosis, and our avoidance of the subject hangs in the air. There's nothing to say, Dad is not healthy; a regular flu could be deadly to him. I hear all sorts of rumors about care being rationed in New York and maybe even New Jersey. So many people in hospitals, younger and healthier ones get the lion's share of attention. The law of the jungle.

I feel useless, sitting in a hospital bed while my mother and Delilah hold my family together. I do just about the only thing I can do: I tell my mother I will pay for everything. If they can bill me directly, great. If not, I'll work it out. Money isn't unlimited in my life by any means, but it's far more abundant than it used to be . . .

In 2015, I won the IBJJF No-Gi Masters Worlds. At that time, it was probably the most prestigious accolade you could have in the world of No-Gi jiu-jitsu outside of ADCC. Not only did I win in my weight class, but I won the absolute division.

The average white or blue belt in the country had no idea who I was. But when black belts saw me in their tournament brackets, they would definitely take a deeper breath. Not only was I a real threat technically, but I was also a UFC and Bellator veteran. I was firing on all cylinders.

Almost as importantly, I had become more of a leader than a fighter. As time went on, I became more comfortable sharing select parts of my past with students, maybe even on social media. I shared my favorite techniques, sure. But I also would just talk sometimes. I would talk to the new student, the cynical blue belt, the over-forty practitioner. These things resonated with people. I found it curious: people seemed to find me relatable, even though in reality I could relate to no one. It was more about how I talked, my accent, the fact that I was a father and on the local school board.

And I liked it. I liked inspiring people. I even started to believe that I was good at it. Other people took notice, too. One of them was a local guy named Todd Shaffer. Todd contacted me out of the blue, asking if I would like to share some thoughts with him for an article on a popular BJJ news site. He would call me and ask me about topics. Some were technical and others were not. But they were all huge hits. Todd was a terrific writer. More and more, people I didn't know started contacting me, writing me, and sharing these articles. It was the first time that I had something akin to a following.

Shortly after, another random person contacted me name Mike Zenga. Mike had a young company he had founded with a few others, most notably jiu-jitsu champion Bernardo Faria, called BJJ

Fanatics. Fanatics was looking to make waves in the instructional market. Instructionals were nothing new, but Mike and Bernardo approached them differently. Typically, jiu-jitsu teachers produced and made their own instructionals. But even world champions had areas that they were great in and others that they were not. Moreover, the quality levels of these instructionals was all over the place. Many teachers filmed on a budget, using poor lighting, sound, and even the design of the course itself. Fanatics had the idea of bringing in many teachers, all under the brand of BJJ Fanatics. Zenga had a vision: Fanatics could be the Netflix of BJJ. Eventually, a student could open a Fanatics app on their phone or television and have all the best instructors in the world which they could select based on their game and what they wanted.

Of course, that was the future, not the present. At present, I was invited to film a pretty straightforward instructional. I suggested teaching my half guard, which had developed into a system of sorts in my head. Zenga invited me to film in Boston, which threw me off. Why not just come to my school here in Jersey? The answer was that they wanted to film in an actual studio. I probably should have been impressed, but I was more annoyed by the inconvenience of it all.

The day of filming itself sucked. It was an hour and a half to the Boston airport, then an hour and a half to the studio. I showed up hungry, tired, and grumpy. The film crew (yes, there was one) was so professional and organized that, for no logical reason, it annoyed me even more. I filmed with them for three straight hours, no breaks. I gave them everything, every secret I had at the time. I walked away proud of it. Even if no one saw it, it was some of my best work.

I ate dinner like a ravenous Viking, paid a cabby a small fortune to get back to the airport, and got home early in the morning, thinking how shitty the morning class at Ocean County was going to be. I was already kicking myself for not asking for cash up front from these guys. Instead, I would get half the profit from sales. I would be pleasantly surprised if I made enough to get my travel fees back. I was kicking myself. What a waste of time. Who even buys DVDs anymore?

A month later, I got my first check from Mike. I stared at it blankly for a few minutes. I set it down on my kitchen counter, made myself a sandwich, and returned ten minutes later. It was still there, and the numbers looked the same. I called Mike and asked him if this was for real or if I was being paid in yen or something. He said it was real. We had sold about $65,000 in the first month.

Just that first check alone was life-changing—so much so that I didn't spend it for a good while, somehow believing that it would all turn out to be a big misunderstanding. But then there was another check, and another. It took months for the shock to wear off and understand that this was not going away. Mike invited me soon to film another instructional. This time, the travel didn't bother me in the least.

It added a third dimension to my career. I had started as simply a competitor, focused on myself and my teammates. I didn't have to worry about anything but training and winning. Then I became a school owner. My first students were mainly training partners, but soon I had students looking up to me, not just as a fighter but as a teacher.

Now, I was not just a teacher but a personality on people's screens. I was a "brand," as much I hate to think of myself that way. I was in some ways really terrible at it. Unlike some people I know, I never had a "persona" or a caricature version of me. Ironically, this worked in my favor. I was authentic, and people understood that.

But there is a dark side. I was famous and normal at the same time. On the street, I could walk around Jersey all day and rarely if ever be recognized. But at a tournament, I could not walk a hundred feet without being stopped. This didn't bother me and it still doesn't. If you see me at a tournament, I will always make time for you. Many people say things like "I didn't ask to be famous," but in my case I essentially did the moment I made those first instructionals. I wanted to share my jiu-jitsu with the world, and I did. Every person that stops me to say hello is a reminder that the community that I belong to has given me so much, the least I can do is stop and talk to every person that wants to talk to me for the rest of my life. It's my pleasure.

What's harder is the people that *don't* want to see me, the ones that only want to criticise and demean. To them, I'm not a real person, just a character. Hating me isn't much different than hating the villain on a show or the rival sports team. Being the object of so much negativity isn't fun. Maybe some people can be impervious to it, but not me.

But the person that hates you is the same as the person that loves you in one important sense: They both write checks in their own way. I can build a house in my Dad's backyard, and my kids can eat. Putting up with some haters is a cheap price to pay.

CHAPTER 31

My father getting sick wasn't entirely a surprise to me. There were early signs before my own run with COIVD started in earnest. Before I was hospitalized, I gave my father enough medicine for a small army. Vitamin C, D, supplements, antioxidants. Everything I had. Living in the same house, you can try and be careful but you can only do so much. We knew he could get sick if I got sick. I told him to be safe and be smart. He did neither. Then again, I'm not sure if I was being safe or smart myself, training in a gym every night with a hundred students.

He didn't take anything I gave him, even after he went from sick to very sick. He was from a different time, a time when you just gutted everything out. This was a guy who had been hit in the head with a radiator, who had walked to the hospital from the freeway after a serious car accident.

While all his ailments, addictions, and being over 65 on top of that, the disease worked its way through him with little resistance. Even a medical team working round the clock would have had their work cut out for them. By the time he was admitted to a hospital, he was clinging to life.

I was discharged a few days later, no longer sick but certainly not healthy. I doubt I could have done a single push-up. When Thomas and Isabelle saw me, they tackled me so furiously I was in pain for the next hour. My hair was overgrown and my face looked like it had aged ten years in ten days. I wanted nothing more than to lie on a couch, get fat, and let my mother take care of me. But the world that I had to now re-enter was one that had kept spinning without me. There was no welcome-home celebration. Instead, the entire focus was on taking care of my mother, the children, and my father—the latter of whom nothing could be done for. Just as with me, there would be no visits.

Everyone needed a different thing. My mother was a rock, unfazed, unwavering. At least that was what she projected. She needed to be occupied. Thomas was barely five; we told him about Grandpa, but it didn't seem to have much of an impact. His energy was undiminished, and he needed as much attention and exercise as always. He was entirely unsympathetic to the fact that I, too, was recovering from a serious illness. He wanted to play, to run and climb all over me. He was physically demanding but emotionally low-maintenance.

We worried most about Isabelle. We had downplayed my illness as much as we could when I was in the hospital, but as soon as she saw me, it frightened her. Even though I was in a somewhat recovered state, her face when she saw me was one of a child understanding vulnerability for the first time—and in her father, the one person who should be invulnerable to her. My voice cracked and wheezed; my skin was pale. My eyes were still puffy from sickness but also tears, which had come on and off for the past few days. She could read me and my mother and understand that we were in distress. We found ourselves having to talk frankly away from her ears when we noticed her staring intently at our conversations. She didn't know what were talking about but could still read our tones, and it scared her.

We can never know when our children will learn about death, decay, and mortality. Parents hope it will be from the death of a family pet, not a person, and certainly not themselves. Isabelle learned it from both her father and grandfather in just a few weeks. I'd like to say she came out stronger, because she did. But in some ways your little girl is never the same.

After about a week, I walked in on my mother in the kitchen. She held a phone to her ear and was nodding to a voice on the other side. Tears were in her eyes as she kept nodding to a person that obviously couldn't see her. I knew as soon as I saw her what she was being told, but she said two words that confirmed it,

"How long?"

It was heartbreaking to hear. My father would lose this fight. He was too old and too weak. But, perhaps most importantly, he had been taken off his methadone for a few days early on. This alone was like a death sentence. Once you're chemically dependent on methadone, you can never stop taking it. He would be transferred to hospice, where they would draw down his food and fluids until he passed away. As my mother relayed this with surprising composure, I embraced her, and we both lost it in the kitchen. We were transported to a time long ago, when we would hug each other and cry over Dad. In this very same kitchen, no less. He had survived so many brushes with death, it's not that we thought he was invincible. More like we had stopped getting emotionally wrecked by the possibility. We had literally prayed over his seemingly dead body before. The man was like Lazarus.

The curse of modern medicine is how long it can keep us alive, well after we should be. Fifty years ago, my father would have passed away in a week. Now, the days ticked on. He spent a week in hospice, then a week and a half, then two weeks. He was more or less asleep during this time, his waking moments never going beyond a basic sort of awareness of the room and its occupants.

I was oddly proud of his survivability. The hospice staff told me they had never seen anybody make it this long. I knew he was tough, and this confirmed it yet again. But other than this small measure of pride, it was torture. Our family lived in a sort of suspended state during this time. I understood more than ever the difference between death and dying. Death is marked by grief, and grieving is a process that will ultimately end. But dying can only bring pain and anguish, because it is ongoing. No healing can begin until death. So the DeBlass family lived in this state for weeks, doing our best to comfort each other. We tried our best to return to our daily routines. Mom went to work, I taught classes, and the kids went back to school. But it was anything but normal. Every time my phone made a sound, I wondered if it was the call I'd been waiting for. When

I reunited with my Mom or even my kids throughout the day, we would search each other's eyes for insight as to whether we were about to get the news. It was like having a gun pointed at your head at all times: you could never truly rest easy as long as it was there.

In the beginning, we said our goodbyes by video—everyone, including the kids. But as the days ticked by, we suffered in the waiting. My daughter began to voice hope that maybe he would get better. I would tell her that Grandpa wanted nothing more than to be with *his* Dad in heaven. I had this conversation with her nearly every day.

One night I discovered Isabelle in the bathroom, crying. She had found her grandfather's cologne and had sprayed it over and over. She sat on the tiled floor in tears, clutching the bottle of cologne like it was a small animal while his smell swirled around the room. I had a long talk with her on that bathroom floor that night, which was the night we filmed her goodbye to her grandfather. I gave her the bottle of cologne, and from time to time I picked up its scent in her room and still do.

And of course, I had my own needs. I hurt myself for the first time in a long while. I heated up a coat hanger with an iron and branded a cross on my arm. I used the exact same spot as when I was sixteen. I wanted to feel pain, as if in doing so I would be sharing with my father. The smell returned, triggering memories from many years ago. Burnt flesh. When it was done, I felt exhausted and relieved, like the physical pain had caused a release. It was short-lived, though, and I did it again shortly after in the same spot.

Dealing with my own pain felt like a luxury I didn't have time for. My primary job was managing my family, my children especially. It was only during the darkest hours of night when I found the time to sit and think. Nights have always been dark for me. I had to remind myself more than once that my children needed me, and that killing myself would only sentence them to a lifetime of pain and trauma that would be squarely on my shoulders. I had to live, but more than that, I had to live happily so that they could know what that meant.

It occurred to me during one of these terrible nights that I myself may not know how to do that. Live happily. Most of my happiest moments came from just that: moments in time. Winning ADCC or Pans, or in Bellator. My happiness seemed tied to my career and my victories. That chapter of my life was coming to a close. I would never win a major championship again.

I wondered if what really fueled me was triumph over adversity. Is that why I had the heart of an old man at thirty-eight years old? Maybe it was time to think of happiness as something that I had gained and could never lose. It wasn't something that I had to re-win over and over again. Perhaps I was attracted to the wild swings of life that most people try and avoid.

CHAPTER 32

I was told that I could finally come and visit the old man. They said he was very close to leaving us but admitted that he had far outlasted any of their original predictions.

As a fighter, I can only compare it to walking into a ring or onto a mat. There are a hundred feelings changing every second, from dread to excitement to fear and then euphoria. Your emotional dial is turned so high that you can't parse out your feelings. It's just raw emotion.

The drive to say goodbye to my father was different. It was like walking into a fight that you could only lose. Not just lose, but lose slowly and painfully.

If they ever give you the opportunity to say goodbye to a loved one, think carefully about it. Often the last thing you see is the most enduring memory. A human who has gone two weeks without food doesn't look like a human anymore. When I entered the room with my father, I thought I had entered the wrong room for a couple of seconds.

He was like a skeleton, reduced to the bare minimum of muscle mass and body composition. I remember his chin bone sticking out maybe a full inch from his lips, an odd detail that stuck with me. His eyes were merely rolled to different sides, and he likely haven't used them for days despite their being open. Half his hair had fallen out, and his body looks like parts of it were literally missing. He was covered in a large robe, and I thanked God I didn't have to see what his body looked like underneath. I will never forget that image.

The one exception was his huge hands, still larger than mine by quite a margin. His knuckles had swelled up over the years, not unlike those of boxers. Some were slanted and cracked from hitting bricks, walls, or people. Looking at them gave me some strength.

I spoke to my father, starting at around five in the afternoon. We spoke until the sun set. We spoke into the night, we spoke long after most of the nurses and doctors had gone home for the night, through the shift changes and the check-ins. He could only groan and moan, but he often did this in response to things I said. It was clear he was aware and listening, at least on some level.

The only message I wanted to convey was that it was okay for him to let go. Stop being so stubborn and let this world go. I told him that I loved him, that he would always be my best friend. I forgave him for all the things he ever did to me. I said that I would take care of Mom, and take care of his grandkids.

Then I played him the videos. From Mom, from Isabelle. From my students and friends. I talk him through each one, repeating the words and the people. He makes noises. Sometimes it feels like he has no awareness of what I'm saying and what is happening, and I lose some hope. Other times, he makes a moan or a grunt at just the right moment to make me feel like he is listening.

I stay underwater for as long as I can, emotionally speaking. But every other hour I come up for air in the form of taking my phone out. Every time I do, there are a hundred messages looking after me, him, my school, my kids, everyone. I respond to as many as I can and keep the world updated on my social media. It's important to share this, and share the pain. Important for others to see that you don't always have to tough-guy it out. But also important for me. I don't need other people's love and support, but it certainly is welcome when it comes. I have the best students in the world. An outpouring of love and positive stories. I let that love rejuvenate me, then I set the phone down and return to my father. Sometimes I read the messages out loud to him.

Unlike when I was in the hospital, staff don't come in very much for a hospice patient. There is far less to monitor. Someone comes in a few times during the night. But other than that, it's just us.

Sometimes it feels like it's just me. I try and keep talking to him, but in the dead of night, when my voice gets raspy and he goes quiet for a bit, we sit in silence. I think about the reality that I am with him now on the last night of his life. I may very well see his life slip away in the next hour, or even minutes.

I have a realization that speaking to my Dad is as much for my benefit as his. It fends of the dark thoughts, like a torch in the night. My Dad had wanted to hear my story, and we had gotten pretty far into it. I didn't regret not finishing it, but maybe regretted that we never got to what it all meant. Which was . . . what?

Maybe I had hoped that I would answer that question through talking with him, come to some sort of peace. And maybe I had started to. I don't know if I had figured it all out yet, but I had gotten this far: everything I had become was because of him. All his darkness and all his love have resulted in a strange mixture that was me. It reminded me of oil and water that naturally separate in the bottle. My father had done terrible things to me, yet he also loved me with all his heart and wanted nothing more than to take back all those things. The oil should have corrupted the water, but somehow they both remained, and I had taken from each of them to become who I am.

"You showed up," I whispered to him. "Maybe not every day, maybe not for every important moment. But you're showing up now, for the last few years. And we're all grateful." I felt like I saw the slightest twitch of his eyes.

CHAPTER 33

I tell myself I will leave at six, around when the sun comes up. I have the thought of watching one last sunrise with him, although there are no windows in our room. Come to think of it, I'm not sure if I've ever really watched a sunrise with him to begin with. He was never really a romantic, and neither was I. I don't say anything to him aloud, but I smile a little thinking to myself that we are finally sharing it now.

My smile only lasts a few seconds, as it prompts me to think about the many things we haven't done together. It's a rabbit hole I force myself out of. Of course, there are so many missed moments in our lives, but that's okay.

I begin speaking, mainly to take my mind off the issue.

"I am grateful for everything we've had over the past few years. We missed a lot before. A lot. But maybe we made some of that up in the end, huh?"

I reach forward and brush his hair, as gentle as if he is a kitten or a piece of porcelain. I stand there for a long while before finally giving him a kiss and leaning in to whisper something in his ear. I pause so close to his face I can smell him and hear his fatigued and shallow breaths. I realize that I don't know what to say. I had said goodbye to him in a hundred different ways in the last twelve hours. I know in that moment, the only thing left is to get up and walk out. I slowly back away from his face as a terrible feeling passes over me that I cannot simply stand up and walk out. It would feel like leaving him. But I also know there is nothing left to say or do.

I sit paralyzed for a few more minutes. When I walk out of this hospital, I will be in a world without my father. As irrational as it sounds, I feel like if I can just stay in this room, he will stay with the living and with me. He won't be able to see or feel or enjoy anything, but he'll still be here.

A thought crosses my mind: *Stop being selfish.* I still need my Dad, but he doesn't need to be here. Not like this. I push my own needs way down deep into my gut. Then I stand up and walk out.

To this day I'm not sure if I did the right thing, although as this is being written, it's not that far in the past. There is no way to say goodbye to a parent that feels right, especially when it involves you walking away and letting them go.

I drive home feeling terrible knowing that my Dad is there, in a hospital dying, and I'm not with him. Maybe I should have lived in that room until the end. But the world doesn't stop moving. I have kids, my mother, and classes starting later today.

I take some comfort in knowing my mother will be driving to see him in a few hours. She has been a rock for the past few weeks, but I know what it does to her suffering in that room with him. She made a vow: through sickness and in health. It was real to her, and she's seeing it through to the end.

I get home around eight. I walk into an empty house, carry myself upstairs. My mind finally remembers that my body feels like shit. I was half dead in a hospital bed just a few days ago; now I've spent the night in a hospital, which isn't much of a step up. I lie down in my bed upstairs.

I dream about my father standing in the bedroom with me. He was leaning against the wall, weeping softly. I sat up in bed and asked him why he was crying. He said nothing but moved towards me. I embraced him and pulled him on top of me, the same way I pull Thomas on top of me. I cradled him like a child, and he was like a child in my arms.

I woke up to the sound of the front door opening and closing. Keys being dropped on the counter, water being turned on. I shifted my body to look at the clock: it was about three in the afternoon. My mom, no doubt, was downstairs. I looked at the corner where my father had been. He wasn't there, but I could still see his outline somehow. I walked down the stairs. My mother was sitting on the couch, staring into nothing in particular. She snapped out of her thoughts and looked at me. Her look was oddly familiar. It was the same look she had given me when my father had been so passed-out on our floor, we had thought he was dead. She and I, we had always been Dad's caretakers. We had a bond over it; we had seen hell together. We had always looked to each other for strength. We would need each other in the coming days.

"He's gone." I am surprised that the words are mine, not hers. It isn't a question, just a confirmation. I can tell by the look on her face.

She swallows, looks as if she's about to say something, and settles on an affirmative nod. I go to her, and we cry on the couch together.

CHAPTER 34

I am, for the most part, okay with sharing my father's death on social media. Not just his death, but his process of dying. I"m fine if people see me in pain. Maybe it will help some people. I get a hundred messages every day from people expressing condolences or grief with me. It's heartwarming and healing.

In other ways, it's not so good.

With every person in my academy knowing about my recent loss comes a total lack of anonymity. On nights like tonight, I want nothing more than to roll into the academy without being noticed. Teach my class, do some light sparring, and have a total escape from life for a few hours. But that's impossible. My life follows me everywhere now. I get a "sorry for your loss" comment every few minutes. And I'm grateful for each and every one. But it keeps the wound fresh and tingling all night. I struggle to stay focused and engaged in the class. My students look at me teaching a technique, but I get the feeling the are sizing up my physical and mental state. My voice is still scratchy and my breathing a bit laboured. My father's death occupied so much of my mental real estate, I completely shelved the issue of my imminent physical decline that the doctor warned me of. I find myself teaching and then transitioning to sparring without much thought, enjoying the routine and the familiarity of it. Something in my head warns me that the routine needs to change sooner than later.

Tonight, I clean the mats in Ocean County BJJ. The building is completely empty. There is a rare silence filling the hollow building, normally filled with people and voices and humid sweat around the clock. Now, my mop echoes across the mat as I dip it into a bucket of water, lift it out, and gradually smear it across the mats. It's freezing inside. BJJ schools don't need heating or even much insulation. I see steam coming from my breath.

I hum an old song my father used to hum. Not even a song, really, just a melody with some words he would throw in that seemed to change every few years. Then, as if I'd caught myself being happy, guilt floods over me. I let myself not think of my father for a while. I imagine his body somewhere, still warm, in the ground, or burned into a billion pieces of dust not one week ago, and I'm humming a tune. What a piece of shit I am.

I start to tear up, but I simply keep mopping and let the tears flow. One at first, then more and more until the tune I'm still humming starts to strain. I stop, barefoot and crying in the middle of my own mats. The million-dollar gym that I own. Headquarters of an empire, and I'm sitting here, ten years old again. I lean against the mat. I don't sob, or wail, or even pout. I just stand there in my own thoughts with my own tears.

My father stood in the corner of the gym, half covered in shadow. I don't know how long he had been there, maybe the whole time. He looked at me with a strange mix of emotion and passivity.

I took a few steps toward him, but some invisible wall separated us, gently nudging me back. My father looked younger, maybe in his forties. He didn't cry but looked like he wanted to, maybe bound by some strange rules of the world he had passed on to.

"Where are you?" I asked.

"I'm in nine one one," he said.

I nodded as if that explained something.

"What happens now?" I said.

"You go home."

"I want to stay with you," I choked out.

He tilted his head as if he didn't understand the statement. "You *are* staying with me."

What he meant by that, I'll never know. He slowly took a step backward, then two.

"If you only knew how much I loved you," he said.

It wasn't the first or the last time Dad visited me in my dreams, but it was one of the few times that it felt like a message.

CHAPTER 35

"Hey I found this on the floor. You would have been kicking yourself if you lost *that* thing," Danielle says.

She drops a wrinkled-up stack of papers on my desk, a stack that had been floating around my life for far longer than it should have: the fight contract with ONE FC. The contract is just a formality. ONE already announced it, and had actively been looking for dates and opponents. COVID had delayed all that, of course. In theory, it gave me more time to train and prepare for my comeback. In reality, it had simply given me a lot of time to think.

"Forget it," I say definitively.

Danielle searches my eyes for a hint of humor. When she doesn't find it, she replies slowly, "So you're not taking a fight?" She asks the question in a way that says she needs an explanation.

I reply with the one word that sums up my thought process for the past few months,

"Why?"

She holds my gaze for a few seconds, trying to decide if she should play the devil's advocate or not.

Before she can indulge me, I say, "I can't think of a single thing I can win from fighting again . . . that I don't already have. The only thing I have left to fight for is my own ego. And I can't be that selfish anymore."

Danielle says nothing, a little surprised to hear me be self-critical. She simply nods quietly. Whether she is agreeing with me or just acknowledging that she hears me, I don't know. She knows about my Dad, my kids. It's time to be selfless for them. It's time to give it all back. My daughter will never cry again because I'm leaving her during a hurricane.

I stand up from the desk and look out at the floor, with the first students of the evening warming up, shaking hands, already starting to workshop different techniques. I think out loud, not taking my gaze off of them.

"There are future champions on that mat tonight. We're going to find them, and when we can't find them we'll *create* them."

"Create who?" Craig Izzo walks in the room, finishing off a protein bar before he changes into his gi for the evening. He asks the question, barely looking up from his phone.

"The people who will take this place to the next level," I reply.

Craig notices my tone and takes a look at both Danielle and me, recognizing that he has stumbled into a serious moment.

"Okay," he says, a bit puzzled.

I help him out, "And that needs to happen with me here, showing up—not fighting across the world."

His eyes change in recognition of what I mean. He simply says, "Okay, then let's go show up."

"Let's go show up," I repeat. I look at Danielle, and so does Craig.

"Let's show up," she says.

I look at the clock. Fifteen minutes until class starts. Craig can start if I take too long making this next call.

"Okay," I say. "I'll call Chatri."

Printed in Great Britain
by Amazon

74391760R00129